Table Of Contents

Introduction

Understanding and respecting the diverse identities of individuals is of utmost importance in today's society. A crucial aspect of this is recognizing and utilizing appropriate gender pronouns. This book delves into the significance of learning and comprehending gender pronouns and their role in fostering a more inclusive and respectful society. It explores the fundamentals of pronouns, their relevance, and the correct usage of various types. Additionally, the book examines the broader social and cultural implications of pronoun usage, shedding light on how language shapes our understanding of gender and identity. Whether you're a student, teacher, professional, or simply someone seeking to enhance awareness and respect for others, this book serves as an essential guide to understanding and utilizing gender pronouns.

Pronouns serve as substitutes for nouns or noun phrases, enabling us to refer to a person, place, thing, or idea previously mentioned or already known. By employing pronouns, we avoid redundancy and enhance linguistic efficiency, as we don't need to repeatedly mention specific names or noun phrases. Pronouns encompass various types, such as personal pronouns, possessive pronouns, reflexive pronouns, reciprocal pronouns, relative pronouns, interrogative pronouns, demonstrative pronouns, and indefinite pronouns. Personal pronouns relate to the individuals a sentence discusses and include words like I, me, mine, myself, you, yours, yourself, he, him, his, himself, she, her, hers, herself, it, its, itself, we, us, our, ours, ourselves, they, them, their, theirs, themselves.

Definition Of A Pronoun

In the realm of language, a pronoun serves as a linguistic substitute for a noun or noun phrase. Its purpose is to reference a person, place, thing, or idea that has been previously mentioned or is already familiar. The utilization of pronouns aims to circumvent repetitive language and enhance efficiency by enabling speakers and writers to refer to entities without repeatedly employing their specific names or noun phrases. Some common examples of pronouns encompass "he," "she," "it," "they," "you," "me," "who," "whoever," "whose," and more.

Why Do We Use Pronouns?

A pronoun functions as a linguistic tool that replaces a noun or noun phrase in speech or writing. It serves as a convenient way to refer to a person, place, thing, or concept. Common examples of pronouns are "he," "she," "it," "they," "you," "me," and "who." The primary purpose of pronouns is to prevent unnecessary repetition and enhance the efficiency of language. By utilizing pronouns, speakers and writers can refer to entities without having to repeatedly mention their specific names or noun phrases.

Different Types of Pronouns

A pronoun serves as a substitute for a noun or noun phrase in language. It allows us to avoid repetition and make communication more efficient. Common examples of pronouns include "he," "she," "it," "they," "you," "me," and "who."

There are various types of pronouns, each serving a specific purpose:

Personal Pronouns: These pronouns refer to specific individuals or things, such as "I," "you," "he," "she," "it," "we," "they," "me," "him," "her," "us," and "them."

Possessive Pronouns: These pronouns indicate ownership or possession, such as "mine," "yours," "his," "hers," "its," "ours," and "theirs."

Reflexive Pronouns: These pronouns are used when the subject and object of a sentence are the same, like "myself," "yourself," "himself," "herself," "itself," "ourselves," "yourselves," and "themselves."

Reciprocal Pronouns: These pronouns express a mutual action or relationship, such as "each other" and "one another."

Relative Pronouns: These pronouns introduce clauses or phrases modifying a noun or pronoun, such as "who," "whom," "whose," "that," "which," and "as."

Interrogative Pronouns: These pronouns are used to ask questions, including "who," "whom," "whose," "which," and "what."

Demonstrative Pronouns: These pronouns point to specific individuals or things, like "this," "that," "these," and "those."

Indefinite Pronouns: These pronouns refer to general or unspecified people or things, such as "all," "another," "any," "anybody," "anyone," "anything," "both," "each," "either," "everybody," "everyone," "everything," "few," "many," "neither," "nobody," "none," "no one," "nothing," "one," "other," "several," "some," "somebody," "someone," "something," "such," "that," "these," "this," "those," "whatever," "which," "whichever," "whoever," "whom," "whose," and "you."

Gender Pronouns: These pronouns are used to refer to individuals based on their gender identity. Examples include "he/him/his," "she/her/hers," "they/them/theirs," "ze/hir/hirs," "xe/xem/xyrs," and more. Respecting and affirming someone's gender identity involves using their correct gender pronouns, making it essential to ask and use them accurately.

Studying Gender Pronouns in the Current Climate

The concept of gender pronouns has received increasing attention in recent years as society recognizes the significance of inclusive language and its impact on individual self-perception and identity. In this chapter, we will delve into the current state of research on gender pronouns and outline the methods to be employed in this study.

While linguistic and sociological research has explored gender pronouns for several decades, there has been a notable upsurge in studies on this subject in recent years. These studies have investigated various aspects, including the use of gender-neutral pronouns, the consequences of misgendering, and the influence of pronouns on societal attitudes towards gender. Nonetheless, there is still much to uncover regarding the intricate nature of pronoun usage, especially in light of ongoing cultural and political dialogues surrounding gender.

This study will employ a mixed-methods approach, combining quantitative and qualitative data. Quantitative data will be gathered through surveys and experiments, while qualitative data will be derived from interviews and focus groups. Furthermore, the study will encompass a diverse sample, incorporating individuals from different age groups, genders, sexual orientations, and ethnicities, with the aim of comprehending the nuanced nature of pronoun usage within varying contexts.

The primary focus of this study will be the current application of gender pronouns in diverse settings, including workplaces, educational environments, and personal interactions. Additionally, we will explore the attitudes and beliefs associated with pronoun usage, as well as the impact of such usage on individuals' self-perception and identity.

Studying gender pronouns is vital for understanding how language shapes societal attitudes and beliefs, while also promoting respect and affirmation for all gender identities. Through the utilization of mixed methods and a diverse sample, this study endeavors to contribute to the ongoing discourse on gender pronouns and their role in fostering an inclusive society.

Now, let us begin by examining the key aspects that underpin the comprehension of gender identity and pronouns. To provide a comprehensive overview, we will present an inclusive list of gender pronouns currently adopted by individuals.

Pronoun Family	Nominative (subject)	Objective (object)	Possessive Determiner	Possessive Pronoun	Reflexive
She	She	Her	Her	Hers	Herself
They	They	Them	Their	Theirs	Themself
Ze/Sie/Hir	Ze/Sie	Hir	Hir	Hirs	Hirself
Ze/Sie/Zir	Ze/Sie	Zir	Zir	Zirs	Zirself
Ze/Sie/Zim	Ze/Sie	Zim	Zir	Zis	Zirself
Xe/Xem	Xe	Xem	Xyr	Xyrs	Xyrself
Spivak 1*	E	Em	Eir	Eirs	Eirself
Spivak 2*	Ey	Em	Eir	Eirs	Emself
Thon	Thon	Thon	Thons	Thons	Thonself
Per**	Per	Per	Pers	Pers	Perself

Masculine	Feminine	Non-Binary	Non-Binary	Non-Binary	Non-Binary
He	She	They	Ze/Zie	Ey	Xe
Him	Her	Them	Hir	Em	Xem
His	Hers	Theirs	Hirs	Eir	Xyr
Himself	Herself	Themself	Hirself	Emself	Xemself

Understanding Gender Identity

In order to foster a more inclusive society, it is essential to grasp the concept of gender identity. Gender identity encompasses an individual's internal perception and understanding of their own gender, which may differ from the sex assigned to them at birth. It is a multifaceted and ever-evolving concept, and some individuals may identify as non-binary or transgender. Respecting and affirming gender identity involves using the correct pronouns and employing language that acknowledges and validates individuals' self-perception. While discrimination and marginalization persist, through education and heightened awareness, we can strive towards a society that embraces and honors all gender identities.

Explanation Of The Topic Of Gender Identity

Gender identity refers to how an individual perceives and experiences themselves in relation to their gender. It encompasses their personal understanding of being male, female, both, neither, or a combination thereof. This self-perception may diverge from the sex assigned to them at birth, as gender identity is an internal and deeply personal aspect of a person's identity.

It is important to note that gender identity is distinct from sexual orientation, which pertains to an individual's emotional, romantic, or sexual attraction to others. One's gender identity does not dictate their sexual orientation; the two are separate and can vary independently.

Gender identity is a multifaceted and fluid concept. Some individuals identify as non-binary, meaning they do not exclusively identify as male or female. Others may identify as transgender, signifying that their gender identity does not align with the sex they were assigned at birth.

Respecting and affirming an individual's gender identity involves using the pronouns and language that they prefer. Misusing pronouns or using inappropriate language can cause harm and invalidate a person's identity. It is essential to acknowledge and honor an individual's self-identified gender in order to promote inclusivity and foster a supportive environment.

While society has made strides in recent years towards understanding and accepting diverse gender identities, discrimination and marginalization still persist. To create a more inclusive society, it is crucial to continually educate ourselves and advocate for the rights and dignity of all individuals, regardless of their gender identity. By working collectively, we can strive towards a society that embraces and affirms the diversity of gender identities and experiences.

Importance Of Understanding Gender Identity

The significance of understanding gender identity can be highlighted in several key areas:

Promoting inclusivity and respect: Understanding and accepting the diverse range of gender identities helps create a more inclusive society that respects and affirms all individuals, regardless of their gender identity.

Reducing discrimination and marginalization: A lack of understanding of gender identity can lead to discrimination and marginalization of individuals who do not conform to traditional gender norms. Understanding gender identity helps to reduce these negative impacts on individuals and communities.

Improving mental health and well-being: When individuals feel respected and affirmed in their gender identity, it can have a positive impact on their mental health and well-being. Conversely, feeling invalidated or marginalized due to gender identity can negatively affect mental health.

Understanding oneself: Understanding gender identity helps individuals understand themselves and their own experiences better, as well as navigate their relationships with others.

Improved communication: Understanding gender identity facilitates better communication and understanding in personal, social, and professional settings, fostering respectful and inclusive interactions.

In summary, grasping the concept of gender identity is crucial for fostering an inclusive, respectful, and equitable society. It not only promotes the well-being and self-understanding of individuals but also contributes to the overall goal of achieving a society where equality and inclusivity prevail.

The Definition of Gender Identity

Gender identity is an individual's personal understanding of their own gender. It encompasses their internal perception of themselves as male, female, both, neither, or another gender identity. It is crucial to recognize that gender identity may differ from the sex assigned at birth and is not necessarily externally visible. Additionally, gender identity should not be confused with sexual orientation, which pertains to an individual's emotional, romantic, or sexual attraction to others.

Respecting and affirming an individual's gender identity involves acknowledging and using the pronouns and language they prefer. It is essential to understand that misusing pronouns or employing incorrect language can be harmful and invalidating, undermining an individual's sense of self and identity. To foster inclusivity and respect, it is vital to use the appropriate pronouns and language when referring to others and engaging in conversations about gender identity.

Distinction Between Sex And Gender

Sex and gender, although often used interchangeably, are believed by some to be distinct concepts that warrant clarification.

Sex pertains to the biological and physiological characteristics that differentiate males and females, encompassing aspects like chromosomes, hormones, and reproductive organs. It is determined at birth based on observable physical traits and has traditionally been understood as a binary construct, recognizing only two sexes: male and female.

In contrast, gender encompasses the social, cultural, and psychological dimensions of being male or female. It encompasses societal expectations, roles, and personal identity. Gender identity, an internal perception of one's own gender, may diverge from the sex assigned at birth. It can manifest as binary (identifying strictly as male or female) or non-binary (identifying outside of the male-female binary).

To simplify, sex denotes the designation assigned by nature, whereas gender reflects one's self-identified understanding.

It is vital to recognize that gender identity is separate from sexual orientation, which relates to an individual's emotional, romantic, or sexual attractions. A person's gender identity does not dictate their sexual orientation.

Respecting and affirming an individual's gender identity involves using their preferred pronouns and language. Misusing pronouns or employing inappropriate language can inflict harm and invalidate their sense of self. Emphasizing proper pronoun usage and language choice contributes to creating a more inclusive and supportive environment for individuals of diverse gender identities.

Explain The Concept Of Gender Identity

Gender identity relates to an individual's personal perception of their own gender. It encompasses how they understand themselves, whether as male, female, neither, or a combination of both. This understanding is deeply personal and internal, and it may differ from the sex assigned to them at birth.

While many individuals identify as cisgender, meaning their gender identity aligns with their assigned sex at birth, others identify as transgender, experiencing a gender identity that does not align with their assigned sex. Additionally, some individuals identify as non-binary, rejecting the exclusivity of male or female and embracing a gender identity that encompasses both, neither, or a spectrum in between.

Differentiating gender identity from sexual orientation is essential. Sexual orientation pertains to an individual's emotional, romantic, or sexual attraction to others, while gender identity focuses on one's internal sense of their own gender. It is also crucial to distinguish gender identity from gender expression, which encompasses how individuals present their gender to the world through their clothing choices, hairstyles, and other forms of self-expression.

Respecting and validating an individual's gender identity involves using the pronouns and language they prefer. Misusing pronouns or employing inappropriate language can be harmful and undermine an individual's identity. Therefore, it is crucial to prioritize using the correct pronouns and respectful language to foster an inclusive and supportive environment for everyone.

Overview Of The Spectrum Of Gender Identities

The spectrum of gender identities encompasses a wide range of diverse experiences. Here are some common gender identities to provide an overview:

Cisgender: These individuals identify with the gender that corresponds to the sex they were assigned at birth. Their gender identity aligns with societal expectations.

Transgender: Individuals who have a gender identity that differs from the sex assigned to them at birth. Some may choose to transition, which can involve various aspects of their life, such as medical, social, and legal changes, to match their gender identity.

Non-binary: People who don't exclusively identify as male or female. They may embrace a gender identity that encompasses both genders, neither gender, or exists along a fluid spectrum. Some non-binary individuals also identify as transgender.

Genderqueer: Individuals who reject the traditional binary understanding of gender and identify as neither strictly male nor female. They may embrace a combination of genders or a unique gender identity of their own.

Genderfluid: These individuals experience changes in their gender identity or expression over time. They may feel different genders at different moments or in varying circumstances.

Agender: People who do not identify with any gender at all. Their gender identity is not tied to male or female categorizations.

Bigender: Individuals who have two distinct gender identities, which can be experienced simultaneously or at different times. They may identify with both male and female genders.

Two-Spirit: A term used among some Indigenous communities in North America. It represents individuals who embody both a male and a female spirit and encompasses diverse gender identities within Indigenous cultures.

It is crucial to acknowledge that each person's gender identity is unique and valid. Respecting and affirming individuals means using the pronouns and language that they prefer. By doing so, we create an inclusive and supportive environment for everyone.

The Importance of Self-Identification

Self-identification plays a vital role in recognizing and honoring an individual's gender identity. It serves as the cornerstone for understanding and respecting one's self-defined gender.

The significance of self-identification lies in its acknowledgment of personal autonomy and lived experiences. It empowers individuals to define their own gender, rather than having it dictated by external sources.

For many people, embracing their true gender through self-identification can be a transformative and empowering journey. It enables them to live authentically, fostering improved mental and emotional well-being.

Furthermore, self-identification is instrumental in fostering a society that is more inclusive and accepting. It brings visibility and validation to marginalized groups, challenging stereotypes and misconceptions surrounding gender.

It is crucial to recognize that self-identification is a complex and ongoing process, unique to each individual. It is important to approach it with respect and openness, acknowledging and embracing diverse journeys and experiences. Additionally, using an individual's preferred pronouns and language is a fundamental aspect of affirming their identity.

In summary, self-identification is essential for understanding and honoring an individual's gender identity. It empowers individuals to define themselves, contributing to the creation of a more inclusive and accepting society.

Explanation Of The Right To Self-Identify

The right to self-identify encompasses an individual's freedom to assert their own gender identity without external interference or coercion. It grants individuals the autonomy to define and express their gender in a way that aligns with their authentic self.

This right holds significant importance as a fundamental human right and is safeguarded by numerous international and national laws and conventions. The Universal Declaration of Human Rights, for instance, emphasizes the inherent equality and dignity of all individuals, encompassing the right to self-identify.

For marginalized communities, including transgender and non-binary individuals, the right to self-identify holds particular significance. These groups have historically faced challenges in having their gender identity recognized and respected. Self-identification becomes essential for them to live in accordance with their true selves and to access necessary rights and services.

It is crucial to recognize that self-identification is an ongoing and evolving process. Respect and affirmation of an individual's right to self-identify are paramount, even if it differs from societal expectations or perceptions.

In conclusion, the right to self-identify empowers individuals to assert their own gender identity, free from external interference or coercion. It stands as a fundamental human right, particularly crucial for marginalized groups seeking authenticity and access to essential rights and services.

Impacts Of Societal Pressure

Societal influence holds considerable sway over an individual's gender identity, exerting both positive and negative effects. Here are a few ways in which societal pressure can impact gender identity:

Societal expectations wield the power to shape an individual's perception of gender identity. From an early age, children are exposed to societal norms and expectations regarding gender roles and behaviors. Consequently, individuals whose gender identity deviates from these norms may encounter challenges in comprehending and accepting their own identity.

The weight of societal pressure can give rise to feelings of shame and isolation among those who defy traditional gender roles and expectations. This is particularly true for individuals identifying as transgender or non-binary, who often face discrimination and marginalization from society.

Furthermore, societal pressure can contribute to the internalization of transphobia and homophobia. Those who do not conform to societal expectations may internalize negative messages about their gender identity and experiences.

Conversely, positive societal pressure can also impact the development of an individual's gender identity. When surrounded by supportive and affirming individuals, there is a greater likelihood that individuals will explore and embrace their gender identity.

These pressures can also influence how individuals express their gender identity. Some may feel compelled to conform to societal expectations in order to gain acceptance or avoid discrimination.

In conclusion, societal pressure carries significant influence over an individual's gender identity, both positively and negatively. It molds perceptions, induces feelings of shame and isolation, fosters internalized transphobia, and affects the expression of gender identity. It is crucial for society to foster an inclusive, accepting, and diverse environment that enables individuals to freely express their gender identity without fear of discrimination or marginalization.

Respecting An Individual's Self-Identified Gender

Respecting an individual's self-identified gender holds significant importance for several compelling reasons:

Firstly, it upholds the fundamental human right for individuals to define their own gender identity without interference or coercion from others. By honoring an individual's self-identified gender, we validate their autonomy and personal experiences.

Furthermore, respecting an individual's self-identified gender plays a vital role in their mental and emotional well-being. When individuals are empowered to live authentically and express their gender identity in a manner that aligns with their truth, it can foster enhanced self-esteem and a profound sense of belonging.

Moreover, the act of respecting an individual's self-identified gender contributes to the creation of a more inclusive and accepting society. By acknowledging and embracing the diverse range of gender identities, we challenge stereotypes and dispel misconceptions surrounding gender.

Equally significant is the fact that respecting an individual's self-identified gender is essential for ensuring equal access to rights and services. When individuals are unable to authentically express their gender identity, they may encounter barriers when seeking healthcare, education, and employment opportunities.

Finally, the use of correct pronouns and preferred language holds immense significance. It not only demonstrates respect, value, and dignity towards the individual, but also fosters an environment of inclusivity and acceptance that benefits everyone involved.

In conclusion, respecting an individual's self-identified gender is crucial due to its alignment with fundamental human rights, its positive impact on mental and emotional well-being, its role in fostering an inclusive society, and its contribution to ensuring equal access to rights and services. Similarly, employing the correct pronouns and preferred language is of paramount importance for these same reasons.

Society And Culture In Gender Identity

The role of society and culture in shaping an individual's comprehension and manifestation of their gender identity is substantial. The following are various ways through which society and culture can influence gender identity:

Societal norms and expectations: Society establishes specific norms and expectations concerning behavior, attire, and presentation based on an individual's gender. These societal norms and expectations have the power to shape an individual's understanding of what it means to belong to a particular gender.

Cultural beliefs and values: Different cultures possess distinct beliefs and values regarding gender, which can shape an individual's understanding of their own gender identity. For instance, some cultures may enforce specific gender roles and expectations, while others may embrace more fluid or non-binary perspectives on gender.

Representation and visibility: Society and culture significantly contribute to an individual's perception of gender identity through the representation and visibility of diverse gender identities in media, literature, and popular culture.

Language: Society and culture also influence the language used to describe gender identities and the pronouns employed. The linguistic landscape surrounding gender identity is shaped by societal and cultural influences.

Societal and cultural pressure: Societal and cultural pressures exert an impact on how individuals express their gender identity. Some individuals may feel compelled to conform to societal norms and expectations in order to be accepted or to avoid discrimination.

In conclusion, society and culture play a vital role in shaping an individual's understanding and expression of their gender identity. Societal norms and expectations, cultural beliefs and values, representation and visibility, language, as well as societal and cultural pressure all contribute to the development of an individual's gender identity. It is crucial for society to foster an inclusive, accepting, and diverse environment that allows individuals to freely express their gender identity without fear of discrimination or marginalization.

Influence Of Societal Norms And Expectations

Societal norms and expectations wield significant influence over how individuals perceive and express their gender identity. The following are a few ways through which these norms and expectations can shape an individual's understanding of their gender identity:

Gender roles: Society often imposes specific expectations and norms regarding the behavior, appearance, and presentation of individuals based on their gender. These expectations shape an individual's comprehension of what it means to belong to a particular gender and can impact how they express their own gender identity.

Societal pressure to conform: Societal norms and expectations create pressure for individuals to conform to predefined gender roles and expectations in order to be accepted or avoid discrimination. This pressure can make it challenging for individuals to authentically express their true gender identity, as they may feel compelled to hide or suppress certain aspects of themselves to fit in.

Limited representation: Societal norms and expectations also influence an individual's understanding of gender identity by limiting the representation of diverse gender identities in media, literature, and popular culture. This lack of representation makes it more difficult for individuals to see themselves reflected in society, thus affecting their understanding of their own gender identity.

Societal expectation of binary gender: Society often upholds the expectation that gender exists solely as a binary concept, comprising only male and female. This expectation creates difficulties for individuals who identify as non-binary or gender non-conforming to express their authentic gender identity.

Societal expectation of gender consistency: Societal norms and expectations commonly emphasize the notion that an individual's gender remains consistent throughout their life. This expectation poses challenges for individuals who experience shifts in their gender identity or identify as gender fluid.

In conclusion, societal norms and expectations have a profound impact on how individuals perceive and express their gender identity. Gender roles, societal pressure to conform, limited representation, societal expectation of binary gender, and the expectation of gender consistency all contribute to the development of an individual's gender identity. It is crucial for society to foster an inclusive, accepting, and diverse environment that empowers individuals to freely express their gender identity without fear of discrimination or marginalization.

Exploration Of Cultural Variations

Culture exerts a profound influence on how individuals perceive and express their gender identity. Varied cultural contexts give rise to distinct beliefs and values concerning gender, thereby shaping an individual's comprehension of their own gender identity. The following examples illustrate how cultural variations can influence gender identity:

Non-binary gender identities: Certain cultures, including numerous Indigenous cultures in North America, as well as cultures in Africa, Asia, and Oceania, recognize more than two genders. These cultures embrace non-binary gender identities such as "two-spirit" or "hijra." Their fluid and non-binary understanding of gender can impact an individual's own perception of their gender identity.

Third gender: In cultures like India and Bangladesh, a third gender category known as hijra is acknowledged as a distinct gender identity.

Gender roles: Diverse cultures may hold varying expectations and assigned roles for individuals based on their gender. Some cultures adhere to specific gender roles and expectations for men and women, while others adopt more flexible or non-binary notions of gender.

Language and pronouns: Different cultures employ distinct terminologies or pronouns to describe gender identities, which in turn shape an individual's understanding of their own gender identity.

Societal pressure: Cultural disparities can also manifest in societal pressures and expectations regarding gender identity. Some cultures exhibit greater acceptance and inclusivity toward diverse gender identities, while others apply more pressure on individuals to conform to traditional gender roles and expectations.

To conclude, culture significantly influences an individual's perception and expression of their gender identity. Cultures diverge in their beliefs, values, expectations, assigned roles, linguistic conventions, and societal pressures associated with gender identity. It is crucial to appreciate and respect these cultural variations, creating an environment that fosters inclusivity, acceptance, and diversity. This ensures that individuals can freely express their gender identity without experiencing discrimination or marginalization.

Impact Of Colonialism And Imperialism

The influence of colonialism and imperialism on shaping gender identities globally cannot be overlooked. The imposition of Western notions and values regarding gender by colonial powers has resulted in the suppression of traditional gender roles and identities within colonized societies. The following are a few ways in which colonialism and imperialism have impacted gender identity:

Suppression of traditional gender roles and identities: Colonial powers often enforced their own beliefs and values on gender, leading to the suppression of traditional gender roles and identities in colonized societies, while simultaneously promoting Western ideals. Destruction of Indigenous cultures: The advent of colonialism and imperialism brought about the destruction of Indigenous cultures and ways of life. This included the erasure of traditional gender roles and identities that were deeply intertwined with Indigenous cultures and societies.

Forced assimilation: Colonizing powers frequently aimed to assimilate colonized peoples into Western culture and values. This often involved the coerced adoption of Western ideas about gender, which resulted in the suppression of traditional gender roles and identities.

Alienation and marginalization: The imposition of Western notions and values on gender by colonial powers has led to the alienation and marginalization of individuals who do not conform to Western standards. This includes LGBTQIA+ individuals and those who identify with traditional gender roles and identities that are unrecognized or rejected by Western societies. Intersectionality: The impacts of colonialism and imperialism on gender identity intersect with other forms of oppression, such as race, class, and sexual orientation.

Acknowledging the historical and ongoing repercussions of colonialism and imperialism is crucial in understanding the formation of gender identities worldwide. This entails recognizing and respecting traditional gender roles and identities, while also acknowledging the imposition of Western ideas and values on colonized societies. Additionally, it is important to work towards decolonization, restoring traditional gender roles and identities, and fostering an inclusive and accepting society that values and respects diverse gender identities.

Conclusion

In conclusion, fostering an inclusive and accepting society necessitates a comprehensive understanding of gender identity. Gender identity is a multifaceted and personal aspect of an individual's identity, often deviating from societal norms and expectations. By grasping the intricacies of gender identity, we can strive towards building a society that embraces and honors diverse gender identities. This entails recognizing the distinction between sex and gender, acknowledging the spectrum of gender identities, valuing self-identification, and appreciating the influence of society and culture on gender identity formation. Furthermore, it involves acknowledging the historical and ongoing effects of colonialism and imperialism on shaping gender identities and actively pursuing decolonization and the revitalization of traditional gender roles and identities. The cultivation of respectful and inclusive language and a society starts with the understanding and reverence of individuals' gender identity.

Summary Of Key Points

In summary, the key points to take away are as follows:

Gender identity is a deeply personal and intricate aspect of an individual's overall identity, encompassing various facets of their self-expression and experience.

It is essential to recognize that gender identity does not always align with societal norms and expectations, as individuals may identify outside of traditional gender binaries or norms.

Understanding gender identity is pivotal in fostering a society that is truly inclusive and accepting of all individuals, regardless of their gender expression or identity.

Differentiating between sex and gender is crucial. While sex is typically assigned at birth based on biological characteristics, gender is a social and personal construct that encompasses a diverse spectrum of identities.

The spectrum of gender identities is expansive, with individuals identifying along a continuum that goes beyond the binary understanding of male and female.

Respecting an individual's self-identification is paramount. People should be acknowledged and honored for their self-identified gender, recognizing their agency in defining and expressing their own identity.

Society and culture exert influence on the development of gender identity, shaping individuals' understanding and expression of themselves through norms, expectations, and cultural values.

The historical legacy of colonialism and imperialism has significantly impacted gender identities globally, leading to the suppression of traditional roles and identities in colonized societies and the imposition of Western concepts of gender.

Addressing the effects of colonialism and imperialism necessitates working towards decolonization and restoring traditional gender roles and identities, acknowledging and revitalizing the diverse gender identities that existed prior to colonization.

Using language that is respectful, inclusive, and affirming is fundamental in validating and honoring individuals' gender identity, promoting a culture of acceptance and equality.

Continued Education And Understanding

The ongoing education and comprehension of gender identity hold significant importance for several compelling reasons:

Firstly, it fosters an environment of acceptance and inclusivity, ensuring that individuals of all gender identities are embraced and respected within society.

Secondly, it enhances awareness of the diverse range of experiences and unique challenges encountered by individuals with marginalized gender identities. This heightened awareness paves the way for more effective support systems and advocacy efforts to address their specific needs.

Thirdly, education about gender identity actively challenges harmful stereotypes and biases. By confronting and dismantling these preconceived notions, we can combat discrimination and mistreatment faced by those with non-binary or non-conforming gender identities.

Moreover, developing an understanding of gender identity enables individuals to gain deeper insights into their own sense of self and personal experiences. This self-awareness contributes to improved mental health and overall well-being.

Finally, striving for continued education on gender identity promotes the creation of a society that is equitable and inclusive. By cultivating an environment where everyone is empowered to live their lives authentically, free from the fear of discrimination, we build a more just and compassionate world.

It is crucial to recognize that gender identity is a complex and multifaceted facet of human existence, continually evolving and transforming. Therefore, it is incumbent upon us to continuously educate ourselves and embrace a deeper understanding of this concept.

Respect And Affirmation Of All Gender Identities

Respecting and validating the diverse gender identities of all individuals holds utmost significance. This entails the conscientious use of appropriate pronouns when addressing someone, refraining from making assumptions about gender based on external factors like appearance or name, and actively fostering an inclusive atmosphere where everyone feels secure and honored. Together, let us collaborate towards the realization of a society that embraces inclusivity and equality for all.

Importance Of Pronouns In Affirming Identity

Acknowledging the significance of pronouns in validating an individual's gender identity is essential, as they serve as a fundamental means of referring to and addressing one another. Utilizing the appropriate pronouns when referring to someone demonstrates our respect and recognition of their gender identity.

Conversely, using incorrect pronouns can generate feelings of disrespect, invalidation, and marginalization for the individual. It can cause discomfort, compromise their sense of safety, and perpetuate discriminatory behavior.

Using the correct pronouns also contributes to the establishment of an inclusive and respectful environment that encompasses individuals of all gender identities. By doing so, we break down barriers and foster acceptance and understanding of the diverse range of gender identities.

Moreover, it is vital to bear in mind that an individual's pronouns may change over time. Therefore, it is crucial to inquire about and honor their current pronouns, even if we were previously aware of their pronoun preferences.

In summary, employing the appropriate pronouns represents a simple yet powerful gesture that affirms and respects an individual's gender identity. By doing so, we actively contribute to the creation of a more inclusive and equitable society for all.

Topic Of Pronouns And Gender Identity

Pronouns serve as linguistic tools used in place of a person's name. They are crucial elements of language and communication, playing a pivotal role in our comprehension and expression of gender identity. English encompasses common pronouns like he, him, his, she, her, hers, they, them, and their.

Gender identity encompasses an individual's internal perception of their own gender, which may or may not align with the sex assigned to them at birth. This multifaceted aspect of human experience is influenced by various factors, including biology, socialization, and culture.

While some individuals' pronouns align with the gender assigned to them at birth, such as he/him or she/her, many others have pronouns that differ from their assigned gender. These individuals may use pronouns like they/them, ze/hir, or any other pronoun that reflects their comfort and identity.

It is crucial to recognize that an individual's pronouns can change over time, and some people may utilize different pronouns depending on the context or individuals involved. Respecting and using the correct pronouns for individuals is essential, even if you were previously aware of their pronoun preferences.

Respecting pronouns is a way of demonstrating validation and respect for an individual's gender identity. Misusing pronouns can make someone feel disregarded, invalidated, and marginalized. Furthermore, fostering a culture where people are comfortable asking for and sharing pronouns contributes to the creation of an inclusive environment that benefits everyone.

In conclusion, pronouns are integral to language and communication, significantly influencing our comprehension and expression of gender identity. By respecting and utilizing individuals' correct pronouns, we exhibit respect and validation for their gender identity, fostering a more inclusive and equitable society for all.

Understanding The Role Of Pronouns

Recognizing the significance of pronouns in affirming gender identity is crucial as it facilitates the acceptance and inclusion of all individuals, regardless of their gender identity. Pronouns serve as a fundamental means of referring to and addressing one another, and using the appropriate pronouns demonstrates our respect and acknowledgment of their gender identity.

Misgendering individuals, by using incorrect pronouns to refer to them, can cause them to feel disrespected, invalidated, and marginalized. It creates an uncomfortable and unsafe environment that can perpetuate discrimination. Conversely, by utilizing the correct pronouns, we foster an atmosphere of inclusivity and respect for everyone, irrespective of their gender identity.

Furthermore, comprehending the role of pronouns in affirming gender identity aids in challenging harmful stereotypes and biases that contribute to discrimination and mistreatment of those with non-binary or non-conforming gender identities. It empowers individuals to gain a better understanding of their own identities and experiences, which in turn promotes enhanced mental health and overall well-being.

It is worth noting that an individual's pronouns may evolve over time, and it is essential to inquire about and honor their current pronouns, irrespective of whether their previous pronouns were known.

In summary, understanding the role of pronouns in affirming gender identity is vital as it promotes acceptance, inclusion, and respect for all individuals, regardless of their gender identity. It also helps combat harmful stereotypes, biases, and discrimination, leading to the creation of a more inclusive and equitable society for all.

The Impact Of Misgendering

Misgendering, which refers to the use of incorrect pronouns when addressing someone, can profoundly affect an individual's mental health, well-being, and overall quality of life. It has the potential to make them feel disrespected, invalidated, and marginalized, amplifying sentiments of isolation, anxiety, and depression.

Beyond emotional repercussions, misgendering can also have tangible consequences. It can hinder individuals' access to appropriate healthcare, housing, and employment, presenting practical challenges. Moreover, it can exacerbate discrimination, harassment, and violence, particularly for those who already face marginalization on multiple fronts.

It is crucial to recognize that misgendering constitutes a form of violence, capable of inflicting lasting trauma and harm. Its impact extends to jeopardizing individuals' mental and physical well-being, fostering feelings of unwelcome and insecurity. Furthermore, misgendering can fuel hopelessness, helplessness, and even contribute to self-harm, suicide, and other violent outcomes.

The occurrence of misgendering often signifies a lack of understanding, awareness, and education surrounding gender identity and pronouns. Therefore, it is imperative that we take the initiative to educate ourselves, remain mindful of the consequences our words and actions may have on others, and consciously prioritize using the correct pronouns when referring to individuals.

In conclusion, we have come to understand that misgendering holds significant implications for an individual's mental health, well-being, and overall quality of life. It perpetuates discrimination, harassment, and violence. It is vital that we comprehend the impact of misgendering and actively strive to employ the appropriate pronouns when addressing others.

Explanation Of The Term "Misgendering"

Misgendering occurs when someone is referred to using pronouns or language that do not align with their gender identity. It can be either intentional or unintentional and can happen in spoken or written form.

It's important to recognize that not all individuals identify within the binary gender system of man or woman. Some may use non-binary pronouns like "they/them," while others may prefer gender-neutral pronouns such as "ze/hir" or "ey/em." Misgendering someone who uses non-binary pronouns is also considered a form of misgendering.

Misgendering can be a manifestation of transphobia and violence, indicating a lack of understanding and education regarding gender identity and pronouns. It can cause feelings of disrespect, invalidation, and marginalization, and contribute to discrimination, harassment, and violence.

To support and affirm someone's gender identity, it is crucial to educate ourselves about gender identity, be aware of the pronouns individuals use, and make a conscious effort to use the correct pronouns when referring to them. Asking for someone's pronouns and respecting them is a simple yet powerful way to demonstrate support.

In summary, misgendering involves using pronouns or language that does not align with someone's gender identity. It can have a significant impact on an individual's well-being and quality of life, fostering feelings of disrespect, invalidation, and marginalization, while also contributing to discrimination, harassment, and violence. Recognizing that not everyone identifies within the binary gender system and being mindful of the pronouns individuals use is essential. By actively educating ourselves, challenging stereotypes and biases, and respecting pronouns, we can work towards creating a more inclusive and equitable society for all, regardless of gender identity.

Negative Effects Of Misgendering

Misgendering individuals can profoundly impact their mental health and overall well-being, leading them to feel disregarded, invalidated, and marginalized. This experience often fosters a sense of isolation, anxiety, and depression, as their identity is not acknowledged or accepted by others. This effect is particularly detrimental for those already facing marginalization, such as members of the LGBTQ+ community.

Moreover, misgendering can evoke feelings of shame and self-doubt, causing individuals to question their worthiness of respect and acceptance. Consequently, this can result in various negative mental health consequences, including diminished self-esteem, increased self-doubt, and even self-hatred.

Furthermore, misgendering can have lasting effects as a form of trauma, severely impacting an individual's mental health and overall well-being. It can engender a sense of hopelessness, helplessness, and vulnerability, potentially leading to self-harm, suicide, or other forms of violence.

Recognizing the detrimental effects of misgendering on mental health and well-being is crucial. By consciously using the correct pronouns when referring to someone, we can actively contribute to a more inclusive and respectful society. Educating ourselves about gender identity and pronouns plays a significant role in fostering understanding, reducing the negative impact of misgendering, and creating an environment that supports the mental health and well-being of all individuals, irrespective of their gender identity.

Impact Of Microaggressions And Discrimination

The impact of microaggressions and discrimination related to pronouns on individuals, particularly those who identify as transgender or non-binary, is significant. Microaggressions, which encompass subtle yet harmful actions or comments directed at marginalized groups, including misgendering, deadnaming, and refusal to use correct pronouns, contribute to a culture of discrimination and marginalization, whether intentional or unintentional.

These microaggressions and pronoun-related discrimination can have severe and enduring consequences. They often lead to feelings of isolation, anxiety, and depression. Additionally, they can result in practical challenges, such as difficulties accessing essential services like healthcare, housing, and employment.

Discrimination tied to pronoun usage also erodes feelings of safety and belonging, heightening the risk of violence and harassment. It further perpetuates a general sense of vulnerability for individuals who are already marginalized.

Moreover, microaggressions and discrimination linked to pronouns foster a culture of fear and mistrust, inhibiting individuals from openly expressing their gender identity. This exacerbates their isolation and marginalization, hindering their ability to access the support and resources necessary for living authentically.

In conclusion, microaggressions and discrimination related to pronouns have a profound impact on individuals, especially those who identify as transgender or non-binary. These experiences generate feelings of isolation, anxiety, and depression, while also impeding access to crucial services. They undermine safety and belonging, perpetuate fear and mistrust, and hinder individuals' ability to openly express their gender identity. To foster inclusivity and equity, it is essential to recognize and address the impact of these microaggressions and discrimination, educating ourselves, actively challenging stereotypes, biases, and discrimination, and consciously using correct pronouns when referring to individuals. By doing so, we can cultivate a more inclusive and just society for all, regardless of gender identity.

Connection Between Pronouns And Gender Identity

The connection between pronouns and gender identity is significant because pronouns serve as a means of expressing and validating our gender identity. Gender identity refers to an individual's internal sense of their own gender, which may differ from the sex assigned at birth.

Pronouns, such as "he," "she," "they," "ze," etc., are words used to refer to individuals and can indicate their gender identity. For instance, a woman may prefer "she" and "her" pronouns, while someone identifying as non-binary may prefer "they" and "them" pronouns.

Using the correct pronouns to address someone is crucial in showing respect and validating their gender identity. Misgendering, or using the wrong pronouns, can make individuals feel disrespected, invalidated, and marginalized. It can also lead to feelings of isolation, anxiety, and depression.

Misgendering is a hurtful act that disregards someone's gender identity. Using the appropriate pronouns is a way to affirm and honor their identity, demonstrating recognition and acceptance through language.

For many individuals, choosing and using the correct pronouns is a vital component of expressing their genuine selves and being seen as they truly are.

Some individuals may identify differently from their assigned birth sex and opt to use pronouns aligned with their gender identity rather than their assigned sex. For instance, a person assigned male at birth who identifies as a woman may prefer "she/her" pronouns.

It's crucial to acknowledge that each person's gender identity is unique and not everyone identifies within the binary gender system. Some individuals may use non-binary pronouns like "they/them" or gender-neutral pronouns like "ze/hir" or "ey/em." Respecting the pronouns individuals use and making a conscious effort to utilize them correctly is a simple yet powerful way to support and validate their gender identity.

In conclusion, pronouns and gender identity are closely intertwined. Pronouns serve as a vital aspect of language and communication, allowing us to refer to others. Using the correct pronouns is essential in respecting and validating someone's gender identity. It's important to educate ourselves on different pronouns, be aware of the pronouns individuals use, and make a conscious effort to utilize the appropriate pronouns when addressing someone. Additionally, recognizing that not all individuals identify within the binary gender system and respecting non-binary and gender-neutral pronouns further promotes inclusivity and understanding.

How Pronouns Are Used To Reflect And Affirm

The utilization of pronouns plays a vital role in reflecting and affirming an individual's gender identity, allowing them to be addressed in a manner that aligns with their authentic selves. When the appropriate pronouns are used to refer to someone, it demonstrates recognition and respect for their gender identity.

For many individuals, selecting and using the correct pronouns holds great significance in expressing their true selves and being acknowledged for who they genuinely are. For instance, a person who was assigned male at birth but identifies as a woman may choose to be addressed using "she/her" pronouns.

For those identifying as non-binary, the use of gender-neutral or non-binary pronouns like "they/them" or "ze/hir" is an integral part of their identity. It allows them to be referred to in a manner that acknowledges and respects their non-binary identity.

It's crucial to comprehend that each person's gender identity is unique and distinct, and it is vital to honor the pronouns individuals use. Misgendering, which occurs when someone is referred to using incorrect pronouns, can be hurtful and invalidating. Using the correct pronouns is a means to validate and demonstrate respect for someone's gender identity.

In conclusion, the use of appropriate pronouns is an essential way to reflect and affirm an individual's gender identity. It signifies recognition and respect for their authentic self. Respecting and utilizing the correct pronouns contributes to the creation of a more inclusive and just society for all individuals, regardless of their gender identity.

Importance Of Using The Correct Pronouns

Using the appropriate pronouns for someone is of great significance as it demonstrates recognition and respect for their gender identity. It enables individuals to be addressed in a manner that aligns with their authentic selves, affirming their sense of self.

When individuals are referred to using incorrect pronouns, it constitutes misgendering, which can be deeply hurtful and invalidating. It not only disrespects and disregards their identity but also contributes to feelings of being unseen, invalidated, and isolated. This impact is particularly pronounced for individuals who already face marginalization, such as those within the LGBTQ+ community.

Using the correct pronouns also fosters a more inclusive and respectful environment for everyone. By challenging stereotypes and assumptions about gender, it promotes a culture of acceptance and understanding.

Moreover, utilizing the correct pronouns plays a vital role in cultivating safe and inclusive spaces, be it in the workplace, school, or community. It helps establish a culture where every individual feels valued and respected, regardless of their gender identity.

Additionally, it is important to note that using the correct pronouns is not only a matter of respect but also a legal requirement in certain jurisdictions. Employers, schools, and organizations are bound by laws and regulations that prohibit discrimination based on gender identity, and adherence to these laws necessitates the use of accurate pronouns.

In conclusion, employing the correct pronouns for someone is an essential act of respect and affirmation towards their gender identity. It contributes to the creation of a more inclusive and respectful environment for all individuals and can positively impact the mental health and well-being of those who have experienced misgendering. It is crucial to proactively strive towards using the correct pronouns, educating ourselves on different pronouns, and remaining open to learning and correcting ourselves when mistakes occur. By doing so, we demonstrate respect and work towards building a more equitable and inclusive society for individuals of all gender identities.

Role Of Language In Shaping Societal Perceptions

The role of language in shaping societal perceptions and attitudes towards gender is highly influential. The words we choose to describe gender and how we refer to individuals can greatly impact the understanding and perception of gender dynamics.

For instance, the binary nature of language, with its reliance on "he" and "she," can reinforce the notion that only two genders exist, enforcing traditional gender roles and expectations. This narrow perspective can be confining and invalidating for those who identify as non-binary or genderqueer. Recognizing and utilizing non-binary pronouns, such as "they/them," serves as a way to acknowledge and respect the diverse range of gender identities.

Language also plays a crucial role in shaping societal attitudes towards transgender individuals. Incorrect pronoun usage or deadnaming (using a name a person no longer identifies with) constitutes transphobia and can cause deep emotional harm. Conversely, employing the correct name and pronouns is a means to demonstrate respect and affirmation for an individual's gender identity.

Furthermore, language can reinforce stereotypes and perpetuate discrimination. Gendered language, like associating specific jobs or roles with "he" or "she," can perpetuate the belief that certain professions are suitable only for men or women. This practice can discourage individuals from pursuing their interests and aspirations, limiting their potential.

In conclusion, language plays a significant role in shaping societal perceptions and attitudes towards gender. The choice of words to describe gender and how we refer to others carries substantial weight. It is crucial to recognize the impact of language on gender, educate ourselves on inclusive language, and consciously make an effort to utilize language that respects and includes all gender identities. By doing so, we contribute to fostering a more inclusive and equitable society.

Creating Inclusive Language Environments

Creating inclusive language environments requires active efforts to ensure that the language we use respects and includes all individuals, irrespective of their gender identity. The following strategies can help in creating inclusive language environments:

Firstly, educate yourself about different gender identities, the significance of pronouns, and the impact of language on gender.

Secondly, employ gender-neutral language by using terms like "partner" instead of "boyfriend" or "girlfriend." Similarly, when referring to individuals whose pronouns you don't know, utilize gender-neutral pronouns such as "they/them."

Thirdly, avoid gendered language, such as exclusively associating "he" or "she" with specific roles or professions.

Next, when meeting someone new, respectfully inquire about their pronouns and make sure to use them correctly.

Additionally, use inclusive terms and refrain from using exclusive or offensive language, such as "ladies and gentlemen" or "normal."

It is crucial to be mindful of your language choices and reflect on the potential impact they may have on others.

Lead by example by using inclusive language yourself and encouraging others to do the same.

Foster a culture of openness and inclusiveness by promoting open dialogues about gender identity and language. Create an environment where people feel comfortable sharing their pronouns and discussing their experiences.

Recognize that mistakes can happen and be prepared to apologize and correct yourself when necessary.

Creating inclusive language environments requires dedication and commitment. However, these efforts are essential in fostering a more equitable and inclusive society for all individuals, regardless of their gender identity.

Importance Of Creating Inclusive Language

Creating inclusive language environments holds significant importance for multiple reasons:

Firstly, it ensures the respect and affirmation of gender identity. Inclusive language allows individuals, including non-binary and transgender individuals, to feel acknowledged and valued for who they truly are, fostering a culture of acceptance and appreciation.

Secondly, inclusive language environments promote inclusion and equity by challenging gender stereotypes and assumptions. They create an atmosphere where everyone, irrespective of their gender identity, feels respected and valued.

Thirdly, the use of correct pronouns and inclusive language positively impacts mental health and well-being. It reduces feelings of isolation, anxiety, and depression that can arise from being misgendered, and instead fosters self-acceptance and improved self-esteem.

Moreover, creating inclusive language environments ensures compliance with laws and regulations. In jurisdictions where discrimination based on gender identity is prohibited, employing inclusive language becomes crucial for organizations such as employers and schools to adhere to legal requirements.

Inclusive language also plays a pivotal role in promoting a culture of acceptance and understanding. By using language that recognizes and embraces diverse gender identities, it fosters open-mindedness and acceptance, leading to more supportive attitudes towards the LGBTQ+ community.

Furthermore, fostering inclusive language environments can enhance productivity by minimizing conflicts, misunderstandings, and distractions that may arise from using exclusionary language or misgendering individuals.

In conclusion, creating inclusive language environments is essential for respecting and affirming gender identity, promoting inclusion and equity, supporting mental health and well-being, complying with laws and regulations, fostering acceptance and understanding, and increasing productivity. It is crucial to actively incorporate inclusive language practices, while also creating an environment where individuals feel comfortable sharing their pronouns and engaging in discussions about their experiences.

Tips For Asking For Someone's Pronouns

Requesting an individual's pronouns is a straightforward means of demonstrating respect and validation for their gender identity. Consider the following suggestions when asking for someone's pronouns:

Firstly, normalize the practice by incorporating pronouns into introductions. When introducing yourself or others, include your own pronouns and inquire about theirs.

Next, opt for a direct approach. Simply ask the person what pronouns they prefer.

To facilitate pronoun disclosure, you can create pronoun buttons or stickers. These items can bear messages like "Ask me about my pronouns" or "Please use my pronouns: [insert pronouns]" and serve as indicators of pronoun preference when worn or displayed.

When referring to someone whose pronouns you are unsure of, employ gender-neutral language such as "they/them" to ensure inclusivity.

Be prepared to reciprocate by sharing your own pronouns when inquiring about others'. This demonstrates a mutual willingness to engage in respectful pronoun exchange.

In situations where someone declines to share their pronouns or if you remain uncertain, exercise sensitivity by utilizing gender-neutral language or postponing the discussion to a more appropriate time.

Lead by example by using your own pronouns correctly and encouraging others to do the same. By doing so, you promote a culture of inclusivity and respect.

Lastly, be ready to rectify mistakes. If you inadvertently use incorrect pronouns, apologize promptly and correct yourself.

Asking for someone's pronouns constitutes a crucial step in fostering an inclusive language environment and displaying respect for their gender identity. It's important to recognize that individuals have varying levels of comfort, so be prepared to adapt your approach accordingly.

Avoiding Pronoun Mistakes

Outlined below are a few methods to avoid pronoun errors and promote inclusivity:

Ask for pronouns: Cultivate the habit of inquiring about people's pronouns upon meeting them.

Use the correct pronouns: Once you are aware of someone's pronouns, ensure their accurate usage.

Normalize asking for pronouns: Foster a culture where it is customary to ask for pronouns and encourage others to do the same.

Utilize gender-neutral language: When referring to someone whose pronouns are unfamiliar, employ gender-neutral language like "they/them."

Embrace inclusive language: Employ inclusive language in both your spoken and written communication, refraining from using terms that may be exclusive or offensive.

Be prepared to make mistakes: Anticipate the possibility of errors and be willing to apologize and rectify them promptly.

Create a culture of openness and inclusiveness: Foster an environment that encourages open discussions about gender identity and language, where individuals feel at ease sharing their pronouns and discussing their experiences.

Lead by example: Use inclusive language yourself and motivate others to do likewise.

Be mindful of your language: Reflect on the impact of your words and remain conscious of how they may affect others.

Be respectful: If someone declines to disclose their pronouns or if you are uncertain, employ gender-neutral language or consider asking again at a later time.

Remember, establishing an inclusive language environment necessitates dedication and effort. It is vital to exhibit respect and understanding towards individuals' pronouns, actively employing inclusive language. Equally important is the readiness to apologize and rectify mistakes promptly.

Conclusion

To summarize, recognizing and validating gender identity is vital for establishing inclusive and fair environments. Pronouns serve as a crucial element in this endeavor, as they validate and reflect an individual's gender identity. The misuse of pronouns, known as misgendering, can have detrimental effects on mental health and well-being. To prevent pronoun errors and foster inclusivity, it is essential to implement the following strategies: asking for pronouns, using the correct pronouns, normalizing the practice of asking for pronouns, employing gender-neutral language, utilizing inclusive language, being prepared to make mistakes, cultivating a culture of openness and inclusiveness, setting an example for others, being mindful of your language, and demonstrating respect. Always keep in mind that creating an inclusive language environment is an ongoing journey that requires continuous effort and dedication.

Key Takeaways

Affirming an individual's gender identity through the use of correct pronouns is essential.

Misgendering can have detrimental effects on mental health and well-being.

Promoting inclusivity involves asking for and using the correct pronouns, normalizing the practice of asking for pronouns, using gender-neutral language, and respecting individuals' pronouns even if they are unknown.

Creating an inclusive language environment is an ongoing endeavor that demands commitment and active engagement.

Continued Education And Understanding

Understanding the significance of pronouns in affirming gender identity is vital for fostering inclusivity and fairness. Pronouns serve as a core component of an individual's identity, shaping how they are perceived and treated. Misgendering, which involves using incorrect pronouns, can profoundly impact a person's mental well-being. To foster an environment that respects and acknowledges diverse gender identities, it is essential to continuously educate ourselves on the significance of pronouns and the consequences of misgendering. By doing so, we can gain a deeper understanding and appreciation for the experiences of individuals whose gender identities may differ from our own. Through this collective effort, we can contribute to the creation of a more inclusive and respectful society that values the identities of all individuals.

Call For Respect And Affirmation

Using the accurate pronouns is a seemingly minor yet immensely influential way to demonstrate respect and validation for every gender identity. To advocate for the respect and affirmation of all gender identities through the proper use of pronouns, consider the following suggestions:

Firstly, make it a natural practice to inquire about people's pronouns when you first meet them. This establishes an inclusive environment where individuals feel acknowledged and respected.

Secondly, ensure you consistently employ the correct pronouns when referring to someone, and take the necessary steps to update your records and address them appropriately. This demonstrates a commitment to recognizing and honoring their identity.

Thirdly, work towards normalizing the act of asking for pronouns by fostering a culture where it is embraced and encouraged. By doing so, you create an atmosphere where individuals feel comfortable sharing their pronouns without fear of judgment.

Additionally, adopt gender-neutral language when referring to individuals whose pronouns are unknown to you. This inclusive approach avoids assumptions and helps create a more welcoming space for everyone.

Moreover, integrate inclusive language into your writing and speech, consciously avoiding terms that are exclusive or offensive. By using language that encompasses diverse gender identities, you contribute to a more respectful and inclusive discourse.

It is important to acknowledge that mistakes may occur. In such instances, be prepared to take responsibility, apologize, and rectify any missteps promptly. This demonstrates your commitment to growth and learning.

Encouraging open dialogue about gender identity and language is essential. Foster an environment where individuals feel safe and encouraged to share their pronouns and engage in discussions. This openness helps build understanding and empathy among diverse gender identities.

Lead by example by consistently using inclusive language yourself. By actively incorporating inclusive practices into your own speech and writing, you inspire others to follow suit.

Be mindful of your language choices and the potential impact they may have on others. Reflect on how your words may contribute to inclusivity or unintentionally perpetuate biases. Strive to cultivate language that respects and affirms all individuals.

Lastly, demonstrate respect by using the correct pronouns even if someone declines to share them or if you are uncertain. Respecting their autonomy and honoring their choice contributes to a more inclusive environment.

In summary, it is crucial to remember that using the correct pronouns is a small yet significant way to respect and affirm all gender identities. By adopting these practices, we can foster inclusive and equitable environments where individuals feel seen, valued, and respected.

The History And Evolution Of Gender Pronouns

Throughout history, the usage of pronouns to refer to individuals has undergone significant transformations. Initially, gendered pronouns like "he" and "she" were employed in ancient languages to differentiate between male and female individuals.

In the English language, the utilization of gendered pronouns persisted for centuries. Nevertheless, during the late 19th and early 20th centuries, there emerged a recognition of the constraints associated with gendered pronouns and a call for more inclusive language. Consequently, gender-neutral pronouns, including "they" and "them," began to be used as singular pronouns in both spoken and written forms.

Over time, the usage of gender-neutral pronouns continued to develop, with the introduction of new non-binary pronouns such as "ze/hir" and "xe/xem" in the late 20th century. These pronouns were specifically crafted to encompass individuals who identify as non-binary, genderqueer, or gender non-conforming.

In recent years, the significance of pronouns has gained increasing prominence within the LGBTQ+ community and society as a whole. Many individuals are actively choosing to adopt gender-neutral pronouns like "they/them" to align with their authentic gender identity and to foster inclusivity.

Furthermore, there has been a growing recognition of the importance of using correct pronouns to validate an individual's gender identity and to cultivate a more inclusive society. Numerous organizations, educational institutions, and companies have implemented policies ensuring the use of accurate pronouns for everyone. Additionally, many individuals are now including their pronouns in introductions or email signatures as a clear indication of how they should be addressed.

In summary, the historical journey and evolution of gender pronouns highlight an increasing awareness of the limitations associated with traditional gendered language. This awareness has propelled the necessity for more inclusive language that respects and validates all gender identities.

History And Evolution Of Gender Pronouns

The exploration of the history and evolution of gender pronouns delves into the shifting usage of pronouns to refer to individuals over time. This encompasses the origins of gendered pronouns like "he" and "she" in ancient languages, the emergence of gender-neutral pronouns in the late 19th and early 20th centuries, and the development of non-binary pronouns in the late 20th century.

The usage of gendered pronouns, such as "he" and "she," can be traced back to ancient languages where they served to differentiate between male and female individuals. However, during the late 19th and early 20th centuries, an increasing awareness of the limitations inherent in gendered pronouns and the need for more inclusive language began to emerge. This led to the creation of gender-neutral pronouns, such as "they" and "them," which started being used as singular pronouns in both spoken and written forms.

The evolution of gender-neutral pronouns has continued over time, with the introduction of newer non-binary pronouns like "ze/hir" and "xe/xem" in the late 20th century. These pronouns were specifically crafted to be inclusive of individuals identifying as non-binary, genderqueer, or gender non-conforming.

The topic also encompasses the significance of using individuals' correct pronouns to affirm their gender identity and foster a more inclusive society. Many organizations, educational institutions, and companies have implemented policies ensuring the use of accurate pronouns for everyone. Furthermore, it has become increasingly common for individuals to include their pronouns in introductions or email signatures, providing a clear way for others to address them correctly.

Overall, the history and evolution of gender pronouns highlight the growing awareness of the limitations associated with traditional gendered language. It is a topic of great importance as it underscores how language can shape societal perceptions and attitudes towards gender. By cultivating inclusive language environments, we can promote acceptance and understanding of individuals of all gender identities.

Furthermore, gaining an understanding of the history and evolution of gender pronouns is instrumental in comprehending the significance of asking for and using people's correct pronouns while also avoiding misgendering. Misgendering can have detrimental impacts on an individual's mental health and overall well-being.

Moreover, it is crucial for individuals to remain informed and keep abreast of the latest advancements in the usage of gender pronouns, as language and terminology pertaining to gender continue to develop. This entails being receptive to learning about newly introduced pronouns like "ne/nem" and "ve/ver" and recognizing that individuals may choose different pronouns at various stages of their lives.

In summary, the history and evolution of gender pronouns emphasize the value of inclusive language and the ongoing need for education and comprehension in this domain. By doing so, we can foster a society that respects and validates the gender identities of all individuals.

Historical Context Of Gender Pronouns

Comprehending the historical context of gender pronouns holds significant importance for multiple reasons. Firstly, it allows individuals to grasp the origins and progression of gendered language, illuminating how it has influenced societal perspectives and attitudes regarding gender. This knowledge provides insights into why certain language is deemed inclusive or exclusive, and how language actively molds our understanding of gender.

Secondly, understanding the historical context of gender pronouns empowers individuals to recognize the vital importance of using correct pronouns. By delving into the roots of gendered language and recognizing the limitations of traditional pronouns, individuals can appreciate that employing the appropriate pronouns is a means to affirm someone's gender identity and foster inclusivity.

Furthermore, comprehending the historical context of gender pronouns equips individuals to approach and utilize language in a more informed manner. By gaining awareness of the developmental trajectory and evolution of gender pronouns, individuals can stay attuned to current advancements in pronoun usage and remain receptive to learning about emerging pronouns and associated terminology.

Lastly, studying the historical context of gender pronouns fosters a deeper understanding of the experiences of marginalized groups, particularly transgender and non-binary individuals, and their encounters with language. By recognizing how language has been employed in the past to marginalize and exclude certain individuals, we can employ language today to forge a more inclusive and equitable society.

In conclusion, comprehending the historical context of gender pronouns plays a pivotal role in establishing a society that respects and validates all gender identities. It serves as a catalyst for promoting inclusivity, understanding, and empathy toward individuals of diverse genders.

List Traditional Gender Pronouns

Traditional gender pronouns, including "he" and "she," have long served as the customary means of referring to individuals based on their perceived or assigned gender. These pronouns, deeply rooted in language and culture, have been widely employed across various languages for centuries, representing the standard way of addressing individuals.

However, the use of traditional gender pronouns rests on the assumption that all individuals can be neatly categorized as either male or female, with "he" and "she" accurately aligning with their gender identity. This perspective fails to acknowledge the intricate complexity and diverse range of gender identities and expressions that exist within society.

Consequently, the utilization of traditional gender pronouns can pose challenges for individuals who do not identify strictly as male or female, or whose gender identity defies the gender assigned to them at birth. For such individuals, being misgendered—referred to with an incorrect pronoun—can be deeply hurtful, exerting negative impacts on their mental well-being and overall quality of life.

Moreover, the reliance on traditional gender pronouns has the potential to reinforce societal norms and expectations surrounding gender, inadvertently perpetuating discrimination and marginalization of those who deviate from traditional gender roles and expressions.

In summary, while traditional gender pronouns like "he" and "she" are pervasive in linguistic conventions, it is crucial to recognize that not all individuals identify with these pronouns. Misgendering can engender detrimental effects on mental health and well-being, while also contributing to the perpetuation of discriminatory practices and the marginalization of those who challenge traditional gender norms and expectations.

Explanation Of Traditional Binary Gender Pronouns

Traditional binary gender pronouns are those commonly used to refer to individuals based on a binary understanding of gender. The frequently employed traditional binary gender pronouns include "he/him/his" and "she/her/hers," designating individuals perceived or assigned male or female gender. These pronouns have enjoyed extensive usage across languages for centuries, establishing themselves as the normative means of addressing individuals.

Nevertheless, the use of traditional binary gender pronouns operates under the assumption that all individuals can be conveniently categorized as either male or female, with these pronouns accurately reflecting their gender identity. However, this assumption overlooks the intricate complexity and diverse array of gender identities and expressions that exist. Many individuals do not identify exclusively as male or female and may find that these pronouns fail to adequately capture their gender identity.

For individuals who do not identify as male or female or whose gender identity diverges from their assigned gender at birth, the reliance on traditional binary gender pronouns can pose challenges. Being referred to using the wrong pronoun can amount to misgendering, a hurtful experience that can negatively impact their mental well-being.

Additionally, the use of traditional binary gender pronouns can reinforce societal norms and expectations regarding gender, thereby perpetuating discrimination and marginalization of individuals who do not conform to conventional gender roles and expressions.

In conclusion, traditional binary gender pronouns, such as "he/him/his" and "she/her/hers," are extensively employed pronouns grounded in the assumption that individuals can be readily classified as male or female. However, it is crucial to acknowledge that not all individuals identify with these pronouns. Misgendering and the reinforcement of societal norms and expectations regarding gender can contribute to discrimination and marginalization of individuals who deviate from traditional gender roles and expressions.

Origins Of These Pronouns

The historical roots of traditional binary gender pronouns, namely "he/him/his" and "she/her/hers," can be traced back to the early stages of language development. These pronouns have been ingrained in many languages, including English, as a long-standing norm. They have historically been used under the assumption that individuals can easily be classified as male or female, with the pronouns accurately reflecting their gender identity.

However, the understanding of gender as a binary construct varies across different societies and time periods. Some cultures recognize more than two genders, resulting in less prevalent use of gendered pronouns.

It is important to acknowledge that the origins of traditional binary gender pronouns are intertwined with patriarchal societies, where men traditionally held more power and privilege than women. This historical context has shaped the development of language that reinforces traditional gender roles and societal expectations regarding gendered behavior.

In recent decades, there has been a growing awareness and acceptance of the diversity of gender identities and expressions. Society has come to recognize that the traditional binary understanding of gender is limiting and harmful. Consequently, a movement towards non-binary pronouns and the adoption of inclusive language practices has gained momentum.

In conclusion, the historical origins of traditional binary gender pronouns can be traced back to the early stages of language development. However, the binary understanding of gender is a cultural construct that varies across societies and time periods. It is important to understand the historical context of these pronouns, rooted in patriarchal societies, which perpetuated gender inequalities. With increasing awareness of gender diversity, there has been a shift towards non-binary pronouns and the promotion of inclusive language practices to embrace and respect the full spectrum of gender identities and expressions.

Societal Expectations And Norms

Societal expectations and norms heavily influence the usage and perception of traditional binary gender pronouns. These expectations and norms are rooted in a binary understanding of gender, assuming that individuals can easily be categorized as either male or female, and that these pronouns accurately reflect their gender identity.

For instance, in many societies, it is deemed "normal" to use "he/him/his" pronouns for cisgender men and "she/her/hers" pronouns for cisgender women. This expectation can exert pressure on individuals to conform to traditional gender roles and expressions, requiring them to be referred to using pronouns aligned with their perceived or assigned gender.

Moreover, societal expectations and norms can lead to the notion that individuals deviating from traditional gender roles and expressions are "abnormal" or "deviant." This can result in discrimination and marginalization of those who do not identify with traditional binary gender pronouns, adversely impacting their mental health and overall well-being.

Furthermore, these societal expectations and norms associated with traditional gender pronouns perpetuate harmful stereotypes and reinforce negative societal attitudes towards individuals who do not conform to traditional gender roles and expressions. For instance, the belief that men should embody "masculinity" and women should embody "femininity" can lead to damaging stereotypes and discrimination against those who do not fit these societal expectations.

In conclusion, societal expectations and norms have a significant influence on the usage and understanding of traditional binary gender pronouns. Rooted in a binary understanding of gender, these expectations and norms pressure individuals to conform to traditional gender roles and use pronouns aligned with their perceived or assigned gender. They also contribute to the marginalization and discrimination of those who do not identify with traditional binary gender pronouns, adversely affecting their well-being. Understanding the historical and cultural origins of traditional binary gender pronouns and the associated societal expectations and norms is crucial in creating inclusive and accepting environments for individuals, irrespective of their gender identity.

The Emergence Of Gender-Neutral Pronouns

The development of gender-neutral pronouns represents a relatively recent advancement in the realm of gender pronouns. These pronouns do not convey a specific gender and are employed to refer to individuals who do not identify with traditional binary gender pronouns. Examples of gender-neutral pronouns include "they/them/theirs," "ze/hir/hirs," and "xe/xem/xyrs."

While the usage of gender-neutral pronouns can be traced back to the 19th century, it wasn't until the latter half of the 20th century that they started to gain wider acceptance. The LGBTQ+ rights movement, coupled with increased visibility and recognition of non-binary and gender non-conforming individuals, has fostered a greater understanding and acceptance of the necessity for gender-neutral pronouns.

In various domains, such as schools, workplaces, and media, the use of gender-neutral pronouns is becoming increasingly prevalent. It is important to acknowledge that not all non-binary or gender non-conforming individuals opt for gender-neutral pronouns, and it is crucial to honor and respect the preferred pronouns of each person.

Gender-neutral pronouns hold significant value in affirming and validating the identities of non-binary and gender non-conforming individuals. They also serve as a means to challenge societal assumptions and expectations regarding gender, fostering a more inclusive and accepting society.

In conclusion, the emergence of gender-neutral pronouns represents a recent development within the history of gender pronouns. These pronouns do not indicate a specific gender and are used to refer to individuals who do not identify with traditional binary gender pronouns. Their usage is increasingly common in various spheres, and it is imperative to honor individuals' preferred pronouns. Gender-neutral pronouns play a vital role in affirming and validating the identities of non-binary and gender non-conforming individuals, while simultaneously challenging societal assumptions and expectations surrounding gender.

Emergence Of Gender-Neutral Pronouns

Gender-neutral pronouns have emerged as a relatively recent development within the history of gender pronouns. These pronouns, such as "they/them/theirs," "ze/hir/hirs," and "xe/xem/xyrs," do not convey a specific gender and are used to refer to individuals who do not identify with traditional binary gender pronouns.

While the usage of "they/them/theirs" as a singular pronoun has been present for centuries, its application to refer to non-binary or gender non-conforming individuals has gained prominence in recent times. Additionally, "neo-pronouns" like "ze/hir/hirs" and "xe/xem/xyrs" have been more recently created as alternatives to traditional binary pronouns. These pronoun sets were crafted by the non-binary and gender non-conforming communities to accurately reflect and affirm their identities.

The rise of the LGBTQ+ rights movement and increased visibility and acceptance of non-binary and gender non-conforming individuals have contributed to a growing recognition of the importance of gender-neutral pronouns. Their usage is increasingly prevalent in various domains, including schools, workplaces, and media. It is crucial to recognize that not all non-binary or gender non-conforming individuals utilize gender-neutral pronouns, and it is paramount to honor and respect the pronouns preferred by each individual.

Gender-neutral pronouns play a significant role in affirming and validating the identities of non-binary and gender non-conforming individuals. They also serve as a means to challenge societal assumptions and expectations regarding gender, fostering a more inclusive and accepting society.

In conclusion, the emergence of gender-neutral pronouns represents a relatively recent development in the history of gender pronouns. These pronouns, such as "they/them/theirs," "ze/hir/hirs," and "xe/xem/xyrs," do not indicate a specific gender and are used to refer to individuals who do not identify with traditional binary gender pronouns. Their usage has become more common in various areas, including schools, workplaces, and media. It is important to respect and honor individuals' preferred pronouns. Gender-neutral pronouns play a significant role in affirming and validating the identities of non-binary and gender non-conforming individuals while also challenging societal assumptions and expectations about gender.

Historical And Cultural Contexts

The origins of gender-neutral pronouns can be traced back to the late 19th and early 20th centuries, a period marked by an increasing awareness and acceptance of non-binary and gender non-conforming individuals. It was during this time that activists and advocates started utilizing "they/them/theirs" as a singular pronoun to refer to those who did not identify with traditional binary gender pronouns.

In the 1960s and 1970s, the feminist and LGBTQ+ rights movements drew attention to the importance of inclusive language and the adoption of gender-neutral pronouns. Activists and scholars argued that traditional binary gender pronouns were restrictive and failed to adequately encompass the diverse range of gender identities.

With the growing visibility of non-binary and gender non-conforming individuals in recent decades, the use of gender-neutral pronouns has also become more prevalent. Communities like the LGBTQ+ community increasingly embrace gender-neutral pronouns as a means to accurately reflect and validate the identities of non-binary and gender non-conforming individuals.

The emergence of "neo-pronouns" such as "ze/hir/hirs" and "xe/xem/xyrs" can be seen as a continuation of this progression. These pronouns were created by members of the non-binary and gender non-conforming communities as an alternative to traditional binary pronouns, and they have gained acceptance as a way to affirm and validate their identities.

Overall, the emergence of gender-neutral pronouns is a response to the historical and cultural context that recognizes the necessity for inclusive and affirming language that acknowledges the diversity of gender identities. It is crucial to emphasize that the use of gender-neutral pronouns extends beyond the LGBTQ+ community, and it is essential to honor and respect an individual's preferred pronouns, irrespective of their sexual orientation or gender identity.

Impact Analysis Of These Pronouns

The impact of gender-neutral pronouns on societal perceptions and attitudes towards gender has been substantial. One of the primary ways in which this impact has been achieved is through the challenge it poses to the traditional binary view of gender, highlighting the diverse spectrum of gender identities.

Traditional binary gender pronouns, such as "he/him/his" and "she/her/hers," reinforce the notion that only two genders, male and female, exist, and that these genders are fixed and unchangeable. However, gender-neutral pronouns, such as "they/them/theirs," "ze/hir/hirs," and "xe/xem/xyrs," enable the recognition and validation of non-binary and gender non-conforming individuals who do not conform to the traditional binary understanding of gender.

The use of gender-neutral pronouns also fosters inclusivity and acceptance. By utilizing these pronouns, we signal to non-binary and gender non-conforming individuals that they are seen, respected, and valued, thereby positively impacting their mental health and overall well-being. It also demonstrates our willingness to adapt and employ new language, conveying openness and a readiness for change.

Moreover, the adoption of gender-neutral pronouns encourages a more nuanced comprehension of gender, challenging stereotypes and societal expectations linked to traditional binary gender roles. It fosters the creation of an inclusive society wherein individuals are free to express their gender identity authentically.

In conclusion, the utilization of gender-neutral pronouns has played a vital role in reshaping societal perceptions and attitudes towards gender. It challenges the traditional binary understanding, promotes inclusivity and acceptance, and facilitates a deeper comprehension of gender diversity. It is crucial for both individuals and society as a whole to continue learning and using gender-neutral pronouns in order to foster a more inclusive and accepting world for all individuals, irrespective of their gender identities.

The Evolution Of Gender Pronouns

Throughout history, the development of gender pronouns has been influenced by cultural, social, and political movements, shaping their evolution over time.

Traditionally, gender pronouns have adhered to a binary understanding of gender, where "he" and "him" referred to males, and "she" and "her" referred to females. However, various movements and communities have emerged to challenge this binary perspective on gender.

During the 1960s and 1970s, the feminist and gay liberation movements advocated for the recognition and acceptance of non-binary gender identities. As a result, gender-neutral pronouns like "they" and "them" were introduced to refer to individuals who do not identify strictly as male or female, or who identify as both.

In recent years, there has been a significant increase in the use of gender-neutral pronouns, particularly "they/them," as a means to validate and honor the gender identity of non-binary individuals. This shift has been driven by the increased visibility of non-binary and gender non-conforming individuals in mainstream culture, as well as a growing awareness of the importance of inclusivity and respect for all gender identities.

Furthermore, new pronouns have emerged in recent years that go beyond the binary system, including "ze/zir/zirs," "xe/xem/xirs," and "ey/em/eir," among others. The use of gender-neutral pronouns continues to evolve, reflecting society's recognition of the diversity of gender identities and the importance of fostering respect and inclusivity for all individuals, regardless of their gender. It is crucial for society to continue learning and adopting new and evolving gender pronouns to create a more inclusive and accepting world for everyone.

Ongoing Evolution Of Gender Pronouns

The ongoing development of gender pronouns plays a significant role in the broader movement towards greater acceptance and acknowledgment of diverse gender identities. As society becomes increasingly aware of the limitations of traditional binary gender pronouns and gains insight into the experiences of non-binary individuals, new pronouns and expressions of gender have come to light.

A notable example of this is the increasing utilization of "they/them" pronouns as a means to refer to non-binary individuals. This shift has been fueled by the heightened visibility of non-binary and gender non-conforming individuals in mainstream culture, as well as a growing recognition of the importance of inclusivity and respect for all gender identities.

Furthermore, novel pronouns that do not adhere to the binary system have emerged. These pronouns, such as "ze/zir/zirs," "xe/xem/xirs," and "ey/em/eir," have been devised to offer non-binary individuals an alternative to traditional binary pronouns.

In addition, numerous individuals and organizations are advocating for the use of gender-inclusive language in general. This entails being mindful of the language we employ and ensuring that it encompasses all individuals, regardless of their gender. This can involve using gender-neutral terms like "partner" instead of "boyfriend" or "girlfriend," or utilizing "they" rather than "he" or "she" when referring to a person whose gender identity is unknown.

The evolution of gender pronouns is an ongoing journey, and as society continues to expand its knowledge and understanding of the vast array of gender identities, it is likely that new pronouns and means of expressing gender will continue to emerge. It is crucial for society to embrace this evolution and strive towards the creation of a more inclusive and accepting world for all individuals.

Role Of Language And Societal Change

The role of language and societal change in the development of new pronouns is a complex and interconnected process. Language is a reflection of society and its values, so changes in societal attitudes towards gender can drive changes in the language used to express and refer to gender.

One way that societal change has led to the development of new pronouns is through the increased visibility and acceptance of non-binary and gender non-conforming individuals. As more and more people have come out as non-binary, the limitations of traditional binary pronouns have become more apparent. This has led to the development of new pronouns, such as "they/them," that are not based on the binary system and can be used to refer to non-binary individuals.

Another way that societal change has led to the development of new pronouns is through the increased understanding of the importance of inclusivity and respect for all gender identities. As society becomes more aware of the negative impact of misgendering and the importance of affirming people's gender identities, new pronouns have been developed to provide non-binary individuals with a way to express their gender that is not based on the binary system.

Additionally, the role of language in shaping societal perceptions and attitudes towards gender is also important. The language we use and the words we choose shape the way we think about and understand gender. As new pronouns and ways of expressing gender are developed and become more widely used, they can contribute to a shift in societal attitudes towards gender, making it more inclusive and accepting of all genders.

In summary, the development of new pronouns is an ongoing process that is shaped by the intersection of societal change, language, and attitudes towards gender. It is important for society to continue to be open to this evolution, and to continue to work towards creating a more inclusive and accepting world for all genders through the use of language.

Significance Of The Non-Binary Pronoun

The role of language and societal change in the development of new pronouns is a complex and interconnected process. Language is a reflection of society and its values, so changes in societal attitudes towards gender can drive changes in the language used to express and refer to gender.

One way that societal change has led to the development of new pronouns is through the increased visibility and acceptance of non-binary and gender non-conforming individuals. As more and more people have come out as non-binary, the limitations of traditional binary pronouns have become more apparent. This has led to the development of new pronouns, such as "they/them," that are not based on the binary system and can be used to refer to non-binary individuals.

Another way that societal change has led to the development of new pronouns is through the increased understanding of the importance of inclusivity and respect for all gender identities. As society becomes more aware of the negative impact of misgendering and the importance of affirming people's gender identities, new pronouns have been developed to provide non-binary individuals with a way to express their gender that is not based on the binary system.

Additionally, the role of language in shaping societal perceptions and attitudes towards gender is also important. The language we use and the words we choose shape the way we think about and understand gender. As new pronouns and ways of expressing gender are developed and become more widely used, they can contribute to a shift in societal attitudes towards gender, making it more inclusive and accepting of all genders.

In summary, the development of new pronouns is an ongoing process that is shaped by the intersection of societal change, language, and attitudes towards gender. It is important for society to continue to be open to this evolution, and to continue to work towards creating a more inclusive and accepting world for all genders through the use of language.

Conclusion

The history and evolution of gender pronouns is a multifaceted and ongoing journey. Traditional binary gender pronouns, such as he/him/his and she/her/hers, have deep historical and cultural roots, but they fail to encompass the full spectrum of gender identities present in our society. In response to this limitation, non-binary pronouns like they/them/theirs, ze/hir/hirs, and xe/xem/xyrs have emerged as alternatives for non-binary individuals to authentically express their gender identity outside of the binary framework. These non-binary pronouns are gradually gaining recognition and acceptance, yet there remains a need for continued efforts to ensure their widespread usage and understanding. Recognizing the historical context and significance of these pronouns is essential in fostering inclusive language environments that honor and validate all gender identities.

Continued Education And Understanding

Continuing to educate oneself and gain an understanding of the historical and cultural contexts surrounding gender pronouns is of utmost importance in fostering inclusivity and respect for all gender identities. By delving into the origins and evolution of gender pronouns, we can gain insights into the reasons behind their prevalent usage in society and the societal expectations and norms associated with them.

For instance, comprehending the historical and cultural roots of traditional binary gender pronouns, such as he/him/his and she/her/hers, helps us grasp why these pronouns have become deeply embedded in our societal fabric and why they are often default choices for referring to individuals. Similarly, by exploring the emergence of non-binary pronouns like they/them/theirs, ze/hir/hirs, and xe/xem/xyrs, we can appreciate the necessity and significance of these pronouns for non-binary individuals.

By cultivating an understanding of the historical and cultural contexts surrounding gender pronouns, we can develop a more nuanced perspective on how language and society shape our perceptions and attitudes towards gender. This, in turn, paves the way for creating language environments that embrace inclusivity, ensuring that all individuals feel acknowledged, seen, and respected.

Furthermore, comprehending the historical and cultural contexts of gender pronouns also highlights the importance of asking for someone's pronouns and using them correctly. This practice fosters a culture of respect and inclusivity, affirming and validating the identities of all individuals, regardless of their gender.

In conclusion, continuous education and understanding of the historical and cultural contexts of gender pronouns are essential for establishing inclusive language environments, fostering respect for all gender identities, and recognizing the significance of using the correct pronouns for individuals.

Respect And Affirmation Of All Gender Identities

Encouraging respect and affirmation for all gender identities through the use of appropriate pronouns necessitates an active commitment from individuals. It calls for self-education on the significance of using correct pronouns for others, initiating conversations about pronouns when meeting new people, and consistently using the appropriate pronouns for individuals in all interactions.

Additionally, it urges individuals to be mindful of their own language use and to strive for the creation of more inclusive language environments. This entails embracing gender-neutral language when suitable and remaining receptive to learning and utilizing newly emerging pronouns.

Furthermore, it implores individuals to challenge societal norms and expectations surrounding gender and actively contribute to cultivating a culture of respect and inclusivity for all gender identities. This may involve advocating for the use of correct pronouns and gender-neutral language in various settings such as workplaces, schools, and community spaces, while also educating others about the importance of using appropriate pronouns.

In summary, a call to action for respect and affirmation of all gender identities through the use of appropriate pronouns is a call to actively educate oneself, employ correct pronouns, and foster an inclusive environment where every individual is respected and affirmed, irrespective of their gender identity.

Using Gender Pronouns Correctly

The accurate use of gender pronouns plays a vital role in affirming and respecting an individual's gender identity. Once someone shares their pronouns with you, it is essential to consistently and correctly utilize them in all interactions. Misgendering, which involves failing to do so, can cause harm and invalidate the person's identity. It is crucial to acknowledge that not all individuals identify within the traditional he/him/his or she/her/hers binary. Many non-binary individuals utilize gender-neutral pronouns like they/them/theirs, ze/zir/zirs, or xe/xem/xyrs. Remaining open to learning and embracing new pronouns is important, while avoiding assumptions about pronouns based on appearance or name. In the event of accidentally using the wrong pronoun, apologize and make the necessary correction going forward. Always prioritize respect and utilize the pronouns that individuals have specifically asked you to use.

Explanation On Using Gender Pronouns

Using gender pronouns correctly involves the practice of using the appropriate pronouns that align with an individual's gender identity. This means using the correct pronoun form, such as he/him/his, she/her/hers, they/them/theirs, ze/zir/zirs, or xe/xem/xyrs, and consistently using the correct pronouns in all interactions. It is crucial to recognize that not everyone identifies strictly as male or female, and many individuals identify as non-binary or genderqueer, which may not conform to traditional binary pronouns. Respecting and affirming someone's gender identity involves using their correct pronouns. Misgendering, or using the wrong pronouns, can be harmful and invalidating, so it is essential to make a conscious effort to use the correct pronouns for everyone we engage with.

Importance Of Using The Correct Pronouns

Recognizing the significance of using accurate pronouns is vital in fostering inclusive and considerate environments that embrace individuals of all gender identities. When individuals are referred to using incorrect pronouns, it can have detrimental effects, causing harm, invalidation, and exacerbating feelings of dysphoria, marginalization, and discrimination. Utilizing the appropriate pronouns is a fundamental act of respect, nurturing a sense of belonging and validation among individuals. Furthermore, it serves as a means to challenge societal norms and stereotypes associated with gender, contributing to a broader movement aimed at fostering greater acceptance and comprehension of gender diversity. Understanding the importance of pronouns and embracing the commitment to using the correct ones represents a significant stride towards establishing a more inclusive and just society for all individuals.

The Importance Of Pronouns

The role of pronouns in language and communication is significant, as they serve as a means to refer to individuals and acknowledge their gender identity. Using the appropriate pronouns for someone is a fundamental demonstration of respect and affirmation towards their gender identity. Pronouns hold a deep connection to the identity of many individuals, and utilizing the correct pronouns can contribute to their validation and affirmation. For transgender and gender non-conforming individuals, the recognition and respect of their pronouns are crucial for their safety, shielding them from discrimination and violence.

Moreover, the use of correct pronouns plays a pivotal role in establishing inclusive and accepting environments. When individuals are addressed using incorrect pronouns, it can lead to feelings of marginalization and invalidation, negatively impacting their mental health and overall well-being. Embracing the understanding of the importance of pronouns and demonstrating a willingness to utilize the correct ones can foster the creation of a more equitable and inclusive society.

In conclusion, pronouns play a significant role in language and communication by reflecting and affirming an individual's gender identity. Their proper use signifies respect and contributes to the establishment of inclusive environments. Misgendering or using incorrect pronouns can have detrimental effects on mental health and well-being. It is crucial to actively make an effort to utilize the correct pronouns when interacting with others on a daily basis.

Role Of Pronouns In Language

The function of pronouns in language and communication is significant, as they are employed to refer to individuals and reflect their gender identity. In English, conventional binary pronouns like "he/him/his" and "she/her/hers" are typically used based on perceived or assigned gender. However, these traditional pronouns do not encompass non-binary individuals who may identify outside the male or female categories.

To address this limitation, gender-neutral pronouns have emerged, including "they/them/theirs," "ze/hir/hirs," and "xe/xem/xyrs," which provide a means of referring to individuals without assuming their gender. The utilization of these pronouns is increasingly crucial as society recognizes the diversity of gender identities and the necessity for inclusivity.

Beyond affirming and reflecting an individual's gender identity, pronouns also fulfill a grammatical role in language by replacing nouns in sentences. For instance, the sentence "John is my friend" can be rephrased as "He is my friend" by using the pronoun "he" in place of the noun "John."

In conclusion, pronouns have a vital function in language and communication by reflecting and affirming an individual's gender identity while also serving a grammatical purpose. The adequacy of traditional binary pronouns is diminishing, and the emergence of gender-neutral pronouns aims to foster inclusivity. Recognizing the significance of pronouns and employing them accurately is essential in promoting inclusive and equitable communication.

Impact Of Pronouns On An Individual

Pronouns hold a critical role in language and communication, serving as references to individuals and defining their roles within conversations and statements. They are a fundamental component of effective communication, aiding in the identification of the subject and speaker. However, the impact of pronouns extends beyond mere linguistic function; they have a profound influence on an individual's self-perception and identity. Pronouns are closely intertwined with one's gender identity, and using the appropriate pronouns is essential for validating and affirming that identity. Conversely, the misuse of pronouns can result in misgendering, leading to detrimental effects on an individual's mental well-being. Thus, it is crucial to conscientiously consider the pronouns we utilize and strive to employ the correct ones when addressing individuals in our lives, fostering an environment of inclusivity and respect.

Impact Of Misgendering

The use of incorrect pronouns, commonly known as misgendering, holds substantial implications for an individual's mental well-being and overall quality of life. Misgendering not only erodes a person's sense of respect and validation but also renders them invisible and disregarded. It can give rise to feelings of dysphoria, anxiety, and depression, exacerbating the challenges faced by individuals. Moreover, misgendering contributes to a profound sense of isolation and detachment, hindering the establishment of meaningful connections and relationships.

The utilization of incorrect pronouns also perpetuates harmful societal norms and prejudices related to gender, further entrenching discrimination and marginalization within vulnerable communities. This misapplication reinforces the notion that gender exists solely within a binary framework, pressuring individuals to conform to societal expectations in order to attain recognition and respect. Non-binary and transgender individuals, who deviate from traditional gender norms, are particularly susceptible to the detrimental effects of this perpetuation.

In order to foster a more inclusive and respectful environment, it is imperative to recognize the impact of misgendering and the use of incorrect pronouns. This involves making a concerted effort to employ the correct pronouns when referring to individuals in our lives and remaining receptive to new pronouns as they emerge. Additionally, it entails becoming an ally and advocate for those experiencing misgendering, actively working towards cultivating a society in which all individuals can freely express themselves and be acknowledged for their authentic identities.

Asking For Pronouns

In creating an inclusive environment, it is crucial to take the initiative to ask individuals for their pronouns. This simple act demonstrates respect and acknowledgment of diverse gender identities. When engaging in such conversations, it is advisable to approach the topic in a casual and non-confrontational manner. One effective approach is to introduce oneself and share one's own pronouns, establishing a comfortable space for open dialogue. It is important to remember that the conversation should not solely revolve around an individual's gender identity, but should instead be part of a broader discussion centered on inclusivity and respect for all identities. Moreover, it is vital to honor and utilize the pronouns that individuals disclose to you, while also being proactive in correcting yourself and others if any errors occur.

Importance Of Asking For Pronouns

In fostering an inclusive environment, one significant step is to inquire about someone's pronouns. This demonstrates an awareness and respect for the diverse range of gender identities. Moreover, it grants individuals the opportunity to express their gender identity and be addressed accordingly, aligning with their true selves. This act of respect holds the potential to positively impact an individual's mental and emotional well-being by validating their identity and reducing experiences of discrimination and marginalization. Furthermore, it contributes to the cultivation of a culture that values inclusivity and fosters understanding, where individuals of all genders feel esteemed and included. It is crucial to recognize that not everyone may feel comfortable sharing their pronouns, and it is vital to honor their privacy and personal comfort levels.

Asking For Pronouns Respectfully

Encourage a norm: Begin by establishing a norm of asking for and sharing pronouns during introductions in both personal and professional settings. This will contribute to normalizing the practice and fostering a sense of comfort for everyone involved.

Lead through example: Take the initiative to share your own pronouns and encourage others to do the same. By doing so, you create a culture of openness and understanding that encourages others to follow suit.

Employ inclusive language: When inquiring about pronouns, utilize gender-neutral language such as "What pronouns do you use?" instead of assuming someone's gender. This demonstrates respect and inclusivity in your approach.

Exercise patience and understanding: Recognize that not everyone may feel comfortable disclosing their pronouns. It is crucial to respect their privacy and comfort levels without pressuring them to share.

Demonstrate respect and use correct pronouns: Once you are aware of someone's pronouns, make a conscious effort to use them consistently and accurately. If you happen to make a mistake, apologize promptly and correct yourself without hesitation.

Avoid assumptions: Refrain from assuming someone's pronouns based on their appearance or name. Instead, adopt the practice of always asking individuals for their pronouns to ensure accuracy and inclusivity.

Cultivate a safe environment: Foster an atmosphere where individuals feel safe and comfortable sharing their pronouns. This entails creating a space that values diversity and respects each person's identity.

Pursue self-education: Take the initiative to educate yourself on various pronouns and their appropriate usage. This knowledge will enhance your confidence and comfort in utilizing pronouns respectfully and correctly.

Strategies For Avoiding Assumptions

To avoid making assumptions about someone's pronouns based on their appearance or name, there are several strategies you can employ. Start by normalizing the practice of asking for and sharing pronouns in introductions, whether it's in group settings or during icebreakers. Another effective approach is to include your own pronouns in your email signature or name tag, setting an example for others to follow. By fostering a culture of comfort and openness, individuals will feel more inclined to share their pronouns and correct any mistakes made.

When encountering individuals whose pronouns you are unsure of, it is best to use gender-neutral language. This demonstrates inclusivity and respect while avoiding assumptions. Additionally, maintaining a learning mindset is important. Be open to new information, willing to make mistakes, and quick to apologize and correct yourself if you unintentionally use the wrong pronouns. This conveys your commitment to growth and understanding, cultivating a more inclusive environment.

Always remember that everyone has the right to their own gender identity and pronouns. It is our responsibility to create an environment that respects and acknowledges this by using the correct pronouns. Through these practices, we can foster a welcoming and respectful atmosphere for all individuals.

Using Pronouns Correctly

Using gender pronouns correctly is an essential component of fostering a culture of respect and inclusivity through language. It is imperative to recognize the significance of using the appropriate pronouns for individuals, as it validates their gender identity and prevents misgendering, which can detrimentally impact their self-perception and mental well-being. A reliable method to ensure the correct usage of pronouns is by directly asking individuals for their pronouns rather than assuming. This can be done in an inclusive and considerate manner, such as introducing your own pronouns or providing an opportunity for others to share theirs. Furthermore, it is crucial to refrain from making assumptions about someone's pronouns based on their appearance or other external factors, and to readily correct oneself in the event of an error. By being conscientious of gender pronouns, we can cultivate an environment that is inclusive and supportive for all individuals.

Correct Usage Of Pronouns

Using the appropriate pronouns to address someone is a crucial way to demonstrate respect and acknowledge their gender identity. Pronouns come in various forms, including traditional binary pronouns such as "He/Him/His" and "She/Her/Hers," which correspond to individuals identifying as male or female. Additionally, there are gender-neutral pronouns like "They/Them/Theirs," "Ze/Hir/Hirs," and "Xe/Xem/Xyrs," which are used by individuals who don't identify strictly as male or female, or who prefer alternative pronouns.

To foster inclusivity and respect, it is important to inquire about someone's preferred pronouns if you are uncertain. Using the correct pronouns in both spoken conversations and written communication is crucial. By doing so, we avoid making assumptions and create an environment that welcomes and values the diverse experiences of all individuals.

Common Mistakes

To cultivate inclusive language environments and honor individuals' gender identities, it is crucial to grasp the appropriate usage of different pronoun types. One common pitfall is assuming someone's pronouns based on their appearance or other factors. Additionally, misgendering, or using the wrong pronoun for someone, is another mistake to avoid. To steer clear of these errors, it is important to respectfully ask individuals for their pronouns and consistently utilize them accurately.

Furthermore, it is essential to educate oneself about the various types of pronouns that are increasingly acknowledged and embraced in society. Traditional binary pronouns, such as "he/him/his" and "she/her/hers," have been widely used, but it is important to recognize that other gender-neutral pronouns, including "they/them/theirs," "ze/hir/hirs," and "xe/xem/xyrs," are gaining recognition and acceptance. By acquainting ourselves with these pronouns and using them correctly, we can contribute to the creation of inclusive language environments that foster respect and affirmation for all individuals' gender identities.

Promoting Inclusivity And Respect

It is vital to always respect and use the pronoun that individuals inform you they prefer, whether it's during introductions or when referring to them later on. If you're uncertain about someone's pronoun, it is important to ask politely and demonstrate respect for their gender identity. In situations where you are unsure of someone's pronoun, using gender-neutral language is appropriate, such as employing "they" instead of "he" or "she." Avoiding gendered language, like "ladies and gentlemen," when addressing a group is also essential.

When referring to someone who identifies as non-binary, it is crucial to use the correct pronouns, even if it may initially feel unfamiliar or uncomfortable to you. Additionally, it is important to refrain from using derogatory language when discussing someone's pronouns or gender identity. Keep in mind that an individual's pronouns may change over time, so regularly checking in to ensure you are using the correct pronoun is essential.

Take the initiative to educate yourself about the various types of pronouns and the experiences of individuals who use them. Being open to learning and understanding will facilitate respectful communication. In the event that you make a mistake with someone's pronoun, be willing to apologize, correct yourself, and proceed with kindness and respect. Leading by example by sharing your own pronouns and encouraging others to do the same helps create an environment that promotes inclusivity and understanding.

Conclusion

In summary, maintaining the proper usage of pronouns is crucial for fostering inclusivity and demonstrating respect towards individuals of all gender identities. It is essential to comprehend the role of pronouns in language and communication, as well as the potential impact of misgendering on an individual's self-perception and sense of identity. To ensure accurate pronoun usage, it is important to familiarize oneself with the different types of pronouns, avoid common pitfalls, and actively promote inclusivity and respect through the appropriate use of pronouns. This encompasses respectfully asking for someone's pronouns, refraining from making assumptions, and consistently using the correct pronouns when referring to others. By employing pronouns correctly, we can contribute to the creation of a more inclusive and respectful society that embraces and affirms the experiences of all individuals.

Summary Of Key Points

Pronouns play a crucial role in language and communication, serving as a means to refer to individuals and establish their roles in conversations and statements. They are not only important for effective communication, but also have a significant impact on an individual's sense of self and identity. Using the correct pronouns is essential for affirming and validating one's gender identity.

Misgendering, which involves using incorrect pronouns, can have a negative impact on an individual's mental health and overall well-being. It can make someone feel disrespected, invalidated, and invisible. Misgendering can also contribute to feelings of dysphoria, anxiety, and depression. Moreover, it can create a sense of isolation and alienation, making it difficult for individuals to form connections and relationships.

To promote inclusivity and respect, it is important to ask for someone's pronouns in a respectful and inclusive manner. This means creating a safe space where individuals feel comfortable sharing their pronouns. It is also crucial to avoid making assumptions about someone's pronouns based on their appearance or other factors. Instead, actively listen and use the correct pronouns that individuals have indicated.

By understanding the significance of pronouns and actively using them correctly, we can contribute to creating an environment that values inclusivity, respects diverse gender identities, and promotes the well-being of all individuals involved in communication.

Continued Education And Understanding

Respecting and affirming an individual's gender identity involves using the correct gender pronouns. Pronouns are not just words in language; they hold deep significance for one's sense of self and identity. Incorrectly using pronouns, known as misgendering, can have detrimental effects on a person's mental health and overall well-being. Therefore, it is crucial to prioritize inclusivity and respect by asking individuals for their preferred pronouns and using them accurately in all interactions.

Avoiding assumptions about someone's pronouns is another important aspect of creating an inclusive environment. Each person's gender identity is unique, and assuming pronouns based on appearance or stereotypes can be hurtful and disrespectful. It is essential to approach pronoun usage with an open mind, willing to learn and understand different pronoun types. Education plays a vital role in promoting understanding and acceptance of diverse pronoun preferences.

Recognizing that pronoun usage is an ongoing process of learning and growth is key to fostering an inclusive society. This means staying informed about emerging pronoun preferences and evolving language practices. By actively engaging in education and understanding of pronoun usage, we can contribute to creating an inclusive environment where all individuals feel seen, respected, and affirmed in their gender identity.

Respect And Affirmation For All

A call to action for respecting and affirming all gender identities through the use of appropriate pronouns involves several important steps. First, it is crucial to educate ourselves on the various gender identities and pronouns that exist. This knowledge allows us to better understand and respect the diverse experiences of individuals.

Second, when interacting with others, it is important to ask for and use their preferred pronouns. By doing so, we demonstrate our commitment to recognizing and validating their gender identity. Using correct pronouns is a fundamental way to show respect and affirm the identities of those around us.

In situations where someone's pronouns are unknown or unclear, it is best to use gender-neutral language. This helps to create an inclusive environment where individuals feel comfortable and respected. It's important to avoid making assumptions about someone's pronouns based on appearance or stereotypes, as this can be hurtful and dismissive of their true identity.

Another important step is to respectfully correct others if they misgender someone. By gently addressing misgendering, we can foster a culture of understanding and promote the use of correct pronouns. It is our collective responsibility to support and advocate for one another's gender identities.

Creating a safe and inclusive environment is paramount. We must strive to cultivate spaces where individuals of all gender identities feel welcomed, accepted, and empowered to express their true selves. This involves challenging discrimination and harassment based on gender identity and standing up against any form of prejudice or mistreatment.

Lastly, we should continuously strive to learn and improve our understanding of gender identity and inclusivity. By staying informed and engaging in ongoing education, we can expand our knowledge and contribute to a more respectful and affirming society.

In conclusion, it is essential to respect and affirm the gender identities of all individuals by using appropriate pronouns. By following these steps, including education, asking for preferred pronouns, using gender-neutral language, correcting misgendering, creating a safe environment, speaking out against discrimination, and continuously learning, we can foster a culture of inclusivity and ensure that everyone's gender identity is acknowledged and respected.

Intersectionality Of Gender And Pronouns

Intersectionality recognizes that individuals face various forms of discrimination and privilege based on the intersection of their identities, including race, gender, sexual orientation, and more. When examining gender and pronouns through an intersectional lens, we acknowledge how different individuals may encounter distinct experiences of discrimination or privilege due to their specific gender identities and how those identities intersect with other factors.

For instance, a cisgender person, whose gender identity aligns with the sex assigned at birth, may not encounter the same extent of discrimination or marginalization as a transgender person, whose gender identity differs from the sex assigned at birth, regarding the use of pronouns. Furthermore, the experiences of a Black transgender woman may differ from those of a white transgender woman due to the intersections of their identities and the unique forms of discrimination they may face.

To foster truly inclusive and equitable spaces, it is crucial to consider the interplay between gender and pronouns. This requires actively seeking understanding of individuals' diverse experiences and how different identities intersect to shape their realities. It also entails actively challenging and dismantling systems of oppression and discrimination that disproportionately affect marginalized groups.

It is equally important to recognize and uphold everyone's right to self-identify and be referred to by the pronouns that align with their gender identity. Respecting and using correct pronouns is vital for establishing a safe and inclusive environment that embraces individuals of all gender identities. By doing so, we affirm their identities and contribute to the creation of a society where everyone feels valued and respected.

The Topic Of Intersectionality

The intersectionality of gender and pronouns encompasses the intricate connections between various identities and experiences that influence how individuals perceive and navigate gender and pronoun use. This concept arises from the recognition that people face distinct forms of discrimination and privilege as a result of the intersections of their identities.

When examining gender and pronouns through an intersectional lens, we acknowledge how different individuals may encounter discrimination or privilege based on their specific gender identities and the interplay of those identities with other factors. For instance, a cisgender person, whose gender identity aligns with the sex assigned at birth, may not experience the same level of discrimination or marginalization regarding pronoun use as a transgender person, whose gender identity differs from the sex assigned at birth. Moreover, an individual identifying as both transgender and non-binary may face different levels of discrimination and marginalization compared to someone identifying as binary transgender.

Intersectionality also recognizes that marginalized groups may encounter distinct forms of discrimination and marginalization. For example, a Black trans woman may experience varying degrees of discrimination and marginalization compared to a white trans woman due to the intersection of their identities and the specific forms of discrimination they face.

Recognizing the intersectionality of gender and pronouns is crucial for fostering genuinely inclusive and equitable spaces. It necessitates actively seeking understanding of individuals' diverse experiences and how different identities intersect to shape their encounters. Additionally, it involves actively working towards dismantling systems of oppression and discrimination that disproportionately affect marginalized groups.

In conclusion, the intersectionality of gender and pronouns explores the interconnectedness of identities and experiences in shaping individuals' understanding and encounters with gender and pronoun use. Acknowledging and considering these diverse experiences and identities is vital for establishing inclusive and equitable spaces.

Understanding How Different Identities Intersect

Understanding the intersectionality of different identities and its impact on pronoun usage holds significance for multiple reasons:

Firstly, it fosters respect for all individuals by recognizing how various identities intersect and influence pronoun preferences. This understanding enables us to honor and validate the identities of each person, utilizing their preferred pronouns and establishing a safe and inclusive environment where they can freely express their gender.

Secondly, it promotes inclusivity by acknowledging the intersections of different identities. This awareness allows us to create spaces, whether in workplaces, schools, or other settings, that value and respect every individual. Such inclusive environments are crucial for ensuring that everyone feels valued and appreciated.

Additionally, comprehending how identities intersect and influence pronoun usage helps us gain insights into the diverse experiences of marginalized groups. It allows us to better grasp the unique challenges they face due to discrimination and marginalization. Armed with this understanding, we can work towards building more equitable systems that address these disparities and promote fairness.

Understanding intersectionality also plays a role in driving social and political change. By recognizing the impact of different identities on pronoun usage, we can actively challenge and dismantle oppressive structures and discriminatory practices that disproportionately affect marginalized communities. This collective effort contributes to the creation of a just and equitable society that upholds the rights and dignity of all individuals.

Lastly, understanding how identities intersect and influence pronoun usage facilitates personal growth. It encourages individuals to reflect on their own identities and consider how they intersect with others. This self-reflection fosters a deeper understanding of the complexities of gender and allows individuals to become more attuned to the experiences of others.

In conclusion, comprehending the intersectionality of different identities and its influence on pronoun usage is vital for respecting and affirming individuals, fostering inclusivity, understanding marginalized groups' diverse experiences, driving social and political change, and nurturing personal growth. By embracing this understanding, we can work towards creating a society that celebrates and respects the identities of all individuals.

Gender And Pronouns In LGBTQ+

Gender and pronoun usage hold significant importance within the LGBTQ+ communities, which encompass a diverse range of individuals identifying as lesbian, gay, bisexual, transgender, queer, and more. Each person within this community may have unique experiences and perspectives on gender and pronouns, highlighting the need to acknowledge and respect these differences.

For transgender individuals, pronoun use is often a critical issue. Many transgender individuals face the hurtful experience of misgendering, where they are referred to using pronouns that do not align with their gender identity. It is crucial to use the correct pronouns when addressing transgender individuals, as this affirms their identity and validates their sense of self.

Non-binary individuals, on the other hand, often use pronouns other than he or she, such as they/them or singular "they." Respecting and utilizing the correct pronouns for all individuals, regardless of their gender identity, is of utmost importance in fostering inclusivity and respect.

Moreover, it is essential to recognize that not all LGBTQ+ individuals feel comfortable disclosing their gender identity or sharing their pronouns openly. Respecting people's privacy and refraining from making assumptions about their gender or pronouns is crucial in creating a supportive and accepting environment.

Within LGBTQ+ communities, the use of inclusive language plays a significant role. Employing gender-neutral terms like "partner" instead of "boyfriend/girlfriend" helps establish an inclusive space that embraces individuals of all gender identities.

Furthermore, it is vital for LGBTQ+ organizations and spaces to prioritize inclusivity by implementing policies that safeguard the rights of transgender and non-binary individuals. This entails using correct pronouns, providing access to gender-neutral restrooms, and fostering an environment that is safe and welcoming for everyone.

In conclusion, understanding and respecting the diverse range of gender identities and pronoun usage within LGBTQ+ communities are paramount in creating spaces that are secure and inclusive for all individuals. By embracing these principles, we can foster an environment that celebrates diversity and affirms the identities of every person within the community.

Unique Experiences Of LGBTQ+ Individuals

The experiences of LGBTQ+ individuals in relation to pronoun usage are diverse and can encompass various aspects:

Misgendering is a significant concern for many transgender individuals within the LGBTQ+ community. This occurs when individuals are referred to using pronouns that do not align with their gender identity. Misgendering not only causes emotional distress but also perpetuates discrimination and marginalization already faced by transgender individuals.

Harassment and violence are unfortunate realities that some LGBTQ+ individuals endure due to their gender identity or pronoun usage. This hostile environment can create fear and restrict their ability to freely express their gender identity or pronouns in certain spaces.

Limited representation and understanding pose challenges for LGBTQ+ individuals in fully embracing and understanding their own identities. Non-binary and gender non-conforming individuals may face a lack of acceptance and understanding, with media and society often failing to provide adequate representation.

Societal pressure reinforces a binary understanding of gender, making it challenging for LGBTQ+ individuals to express their gender identity or pronouns authentically. This pressure may lead to fear of rejection, harassment, and the expectation to conform to societal norms.

Coming out as transgender or non-binary can be an emotionally demanding process for many LGBTQ+ individuals. It involves disclosing one's gender identity and preferred pronouns, and the reactions received can range from acceptance to rejection.

Respecting privacy is crucial as many LGBTQ+ individuals may not feel comfortable sharing their pronouns or gender identity with others. Concerns about safety and acceptance may prevent individuals from coming out. It is important to honor their privacy and refrain from making assumptions about their gender or pronouns.

In conclusion, LGBTQ+ individuals face unique experiences related to pronoun usage influenced by societal pressure, discrimination, and marginalization. Understanding and respecting these experiences are essential in fostering a safe and inclusive environment that celebrates the diversity within the LGBTQ+ community.

Significance Of Non-Binary Pronouns

Non-binary pronouns, such as "they/them" and "ze/hir," hold a significant historical and cultural value within LGBTQ+ communities.

The usage of "they/them" as a non-binary pronoun can be traced back to the 16th century when it was commonly employed as a singular pronoun. However, it gained particular traction in the 20th century within LGBTQ+ communities as a means for individuals who don't identify strictly as male or female to express their gender identity.

Similarly, "ze/hir" and other invented pronouns emerged as alternatives used by those identifying as non-binary, genderqueer, or other non-binary identities. These pronouns provide a means for individuals who feel uncomfortable with traditional pronouns to express their gender identity more authentically.

The use of non-binary pronouns holds significance for LGBTQ+ communities as it empowers individuals to express their gender identity in a way that resonates with their true selves. It also challenges societal norms surrounding gender and pronoun usage, fostering a more inclusive and equitable environment for all individuals.

Non-binary pronouns can be viewed as acts of resistance and resilience against a society that predominantly recognizes and validates binary gender identities and expressions. They serve to defy the societal expectation that one's gender must be immediately recognizable or conform to a binary framework. By offering individuals the freedom to express their gender identity genuinely, non-binary pronouns challenge discrimination and marginalization. They empower individuals to assert their right to self-identify and be acknowledged in a manner that aligns with their gender identity. Consequently, non-binary pronouns become a powerful tool for promoting acceptance, understanding, and equality within LGBTQ+ communities and society at large.

Impact Of Discrimination And Marginalization

Discrimination and marginalization profoundly affect pronoun usage within LGBTQ+ communities, manifesting in various ways:

Fear of misgendering: Discrimination and marginalization generate a fear of being misgendered, where individuals are addressed with pronouns that don't align with their gender identity. This fear can lead to individuals refraining from expressing their preferred pronouns or avoiding certain spaces to evade misgendering.

Harassment and violence: Discrimination and marginalization also contribute to instances of harassment and violence based on gender identity or pronoun usage. This pervasive threat hinders individuals from feeling safe in expressing their gender identity or pronouns, even within spaces intended to be secure and inclusive.

Limited representation and understanding: Discrimination and marginalization obstruct comprehensive representation and understanding of LGBTQ+ identities and experiences. This obstacle makes it challenging for individuals to access resources and support, while also perpetuating a lack of comprehension and acceptance towards non-binary and gender non-conforming individuals.

Societal pressure: Discrimination and marginalization reinforce societal pressure to conform to binary gender norms. This pressure complicates the ability of LGBTQ+ individuals to authentically express their gender identity or pronouns, often leading to a sense of having to conceal or suppress their true selves.

Coming out: Coming out can be an arduous and emotional process for some LGBTQ+ individuals. Discrimination and marginalization further exacerbate these difficulties, as individuals may experience heightened fears of rejection or harassment during this vulnerable time.

Recognizing the impact of discrimination and marginalization on pronoun usage within LGBTQ+ communities is vital. It is crucial for society to actively foster a more inclusive and equitable environment for all individuals by promoting education and awareness, establishing policies and laws that safeguard the rights of LGBTQ+ individuals, and cultivating a culture of acceptance and respect for diverse gender identities and expressions.

Moreover, empowering LGBTQ+ communities to create their own safe spaces where they can freely express themselves and educate others about the significance of pronoun usage and the consequences of discrimination and marginalization is equally important.

In conclusion, understanding and acknowledging the repercussions of discrimination and marginalization on pronoun usage within LGBTQ+ communities is pivotal to the creation of a more inclusive and equitable society. Society must take proactive measures to combat discrimination and marginalization, while supporting and empowering LGBTQ+ individuals in their journey towards authentic self-expression.

Pronouns And Disability

When it comes to individuals with disabilities, it is crucial to be mindful and supportive of their mental well-being through the use of correct gender pronouns. Here are some considerations to keep in mind:

Communication challenges: Not all individuals with disabilities are able to communicate their preferred pronouns. Verbal limitations or difficulties expressing themselves may hinder their ability to convey pronoun preferences. It is important to avoid assumptions based on their disability and be sensitive to this aspect.

Fluidity of pronouns: Some individuals with disabilities may use different pronouns at different times or have multiple preferred pronouns. Flexibility in using the correct pronouns and being aware of potential changes is key to respectful and inclusive communication.

Understanding and memory: Some individuals with disabilities may experience challenges in understanding or remembering pronouns. It is important to exercise patience and utilize clear language when discussing pronouns with them to ensure mutual understanding.

Social cues: Individuals with disabilities may have difficulty picking up on social cues and may not realize when they are being misgendered. Providing explicit and direct feedback is essential, as expecting them to understand social cues may not be effective in these situations.

Heightened discrimination and marginalization: Some individuals with disabilities may face increased discrimination and marginalization related to their gender identity. It is crucial to acknowledge this reality and actively work towards creating an environment that is inclusive and equitable for all individuals.

Accommodations for disability: Accommodations play a vital role in pronoun usage for individuals with disabilities. Some may require written or visual aids to comprehend and remember pronouns effectively. Ensuring proper disability accommodations is important to promote understanding and respectful communication.

Respecting self-identification: Regardless of an individual's disability, it is imperative to honor their right to self-identify and use the pronouns they prefer. Every person deserves the opportunity to express their gender identity in an authentic manner.

In conclusion, it is essential to recognize the unique experiences and requirements of individuals with disabilities in terms of pronoun usage. Respecting their pronoun preferences, being mindful and adaptable, and actively fostering an inclusive and equitable environment are all crucial steps in promoting respectful communication and support for all individuals, regardless of disability.

Impact Of Disabilities On Pronoun Usage

The impact of disabilities on pronoun usage and communication is significant and should be acknowledged. Here are some key aspects to consider:

Challenges in communicating preferred pronouns: Some individuals with disabilities may struggle to communicate their preferred pronouns due to limitations in verbal skills or expressing themselves. This poses difficulties for others in correctly using their preferred pronouns.

Understanding and remembering pronouns: Certain disabilities can hinder the comprehension and recollection of pronouns. This can result in confusion and misgendering, causing distress for the individual.

Heightened discrimination and marginalization: Individuals with disabilities may face increased discrimination and marginalization regarding their gender identity. This creates barriers to expressing their gender identity and being acknowledged accordingly.

Difficulties with social cues: Some individuals with disabilities may have challenges understanding social cues and may not recognize when they are being misgendered. This makes it challenging for them to correct others in such situations.

Accommodations: Individuals with disabilities may require accommodations, such as written or visual aids, to understand and remember pronouns. It is essential to ensure that necessary accommodations are provided to those who need them.

Self-identification: It is crucial to uphold the right of every individual to self-identify and use their preferred pronouns, regardless of disability. Making assumptions about pronouns based on someone's disability is inappropriate, and individuals should have the freedom to express their gender identity authentically.

Society must be aware of the impact disabilities have on pronoun usage and communication and actively strive to create an inclusive and equitable environment for individuals with disabilities. This can be achieved through education, raising awareness, implementing policies and laws safeguarding the rights of individuals with disabilities, and fostering a culture of acceptance and respect for all, regardless of their abilities.

Furthermore, support systems such as counseling, peer support groups, and specialized education programs play a crucial role in assisting individuals with disabilities, especially those who are part of the LGBTQ+ communities, in navigating the complexities of pronoun usage and communication.

In conclusion, disabilities have a significant influence on pronoun usage and communication. Society needs to acknowledge and address these challenges, promoting inclusivity and equity for individuals with disabilities. Supporting individuals with disabilities in expressing their authentic selves and respecting their right to self-identify are key steps towards a more inclusive society.

Importance Of Accommodating Disabilities

Creating a society that is inclusive and equitable requires accommodating the needs and preferences of individuals with disabilities. These individuals often face unique challenges that can affect their ability to express their gender identity and be acknowledged accordingly.

A fundamental approach to accommodation involves providing aids, such as written or visual materials, to help individuals with disabilities understand and remember pronouns. This reduces confusion and the likelihood of misgendering, facilitating a smoother expression of their gender identity.

Another crucial aspect of accommodation is the establishment of policies and laws that safeguard the rights of individuals with disabilities. These legal measures should prohibit discrimination based on disability and ensure equal access to opportunities and services for all individuals, regardless of their disabilities.

Fostering a culture of acceptance and respect for all individuals, irrespective of their abilities, is equally important. This can be achieved through education and raising awareness about disability inclusion. Additionally, creating safe spaces where individuals with disabilities can freely express themselves and receive recognition for who they are contributes to fostering this culture of acceptance.

In conclusion, accommodating the needs and preferences of individuals with disabilities plays a vital role in building an inclusive and equitable society. It necessitates providing appropriate aids, enacting protective policies and laws, and nurturing a culture that embraces and respects individuals of all abilities.

Role Of Accessibility In Pronoun Usage

Pronoun usage and accessibility are deeply interconnected, as they ensure that individuals with disabilities have equitable access to information and resources pertaining to pronouns, enabling them to express their gender identity according to their preferences.

One effective way to incorporate accessibility into pronoun usage is by providing written or visual aids. These aids can assist individuals with disabilities in understanding and remembering pronouns. Examples include pronoun buttons, name tags, guides, or cheat sheets that offer visual support and guidance.

Moreover, ensuring accessibility involves providing alternative communication methods for individuals with disabilities who may have difficulty with conventional modes of communication. This can involve sign language interpretation or the use of assistive technologies, empowering individuals to express their preferred pronouns and be acknowledged in alignment with their gender identity.

When crafting policies and laws, it is crucial to consider the accessibility needs of individuals with disabilities. These measures should encompass protections against disability-based discrimination and guarantee equal opportunities and services for everyone, regardless of their disabilities.

In conclusion, accessibility plays a vital role in pronoun usage by ensuring that individuals with disabilities have equal access to information and resources related to pronouns, enabling them to express their gender identity in a manner that respects their preferences. Incorporating written or visual aids, alternative communication methods, and inclusive policies are essential steps toward fostering accessible pronoun usage.

Pronouns And Race

The connection between pronouns and race is multifaceted and warrants attention. One aspect where race influences pronoun usage is through the cultural and linguistic diversity found among different racial groups. For instance, many Indigenous cultures embrace multiple gender systems that encompass non-binary identities and pronouns, sometimes lacking direct translations for binary pronouns like "he" or "she."

Another way in which race can impact pronoun usage is through experiences of racial discrimination and marginalization. Individuals from marginalized racial groups may face a higher likelihood of encountering misgendering and discrimination based on their pronoun usage. Consequently, expressing their gender identity and receiving recognition that aligns with it can become challenging.

Furthermore, racial and ethnic minority groups may possess their own linguistic and cultural pronouns. This extends not only within their own communities but also within the languages they speak and the cultures they belong to. For example, certain African languages lack gendered pronouns altogether, while others include multiple gendered pronouns.

It is crucial for society to acknowledge and appreciate the cultural and linguistic diversity present among various racial groups. Actively striving to establish an inclusive and equitable environment for individuals of all races is essential. Achieving this requires education, raising awareness, developing policies and laws that safeguard the rights of people from all racial backgrounds, and fostering a culture characterized by acceptance and respect for every individual, regardless of their race.

In conclusion, the interplay between pronouns and race necessitates an understanding of the cultural and linguistic diversity within different racial groups, as well as the experiences of racial discrimination and marginalization. Taking active measures to cultivate inclusivity and equity for individuals of all races through education, policies, and the promotion of acceptance and respect is of utmost importance.

Intersection Of Race And Pronoun Usage

The relationship between race and pronoun usage emphasizes how different identities and experiences can intersect, affecting an individual's capacity to express their gender identity and be acknowledged in a manner that aligns with it.

For individuals belonging to marginalized racial groups, the experience of racial discrimination and marginalization can compound the challenges associated with misgendering and discrimination based on pronoun usage. This compound effect further complicates their ability to express their gender identity and be recognized accordingly.

Furthermore, many racial and ethnic minority cultures possess their own linguistic and cultural pronouns, not only within their own communities but also in the languages they speak and the cultures they originate from. For instance, some African languages lack gendered pronouns, while others embrace multiple gendered pronouns. Consequently, individuals from these cultures may face difficulty expressing their gender identity using the binary pronouns commonly recognized in Western cultures.

Recognizing and understanding the distinct experiences and obstacles encountered by individuals from marginalized racial groups regarding pronoun usage is essential. This entails being more mindful of the cultural and linguistic diversity within different racial groups and actively striving to establish an inclusive and equitable environment for individuals of all races. This can be accomplished through education, raising awareness, enacting policies and laws that safeguard the rights of individuals from all racial backgrounds, and cultivating a culture characterized by acceptance and respect for every individual, regardless of their race.

In conclusion, the intersection of race and pronoun usage underscores the interconnectedness of diverse identities and experiences, which influence an individual's ability to express their gender identity. Recognizing and understanding the unique experiences and challenges faced by individuals from marginalized racial groups in pronoun usage is crucial, as is actively working to create an inclusive and equitable environment for individuals of all races.

Systemic Racism And Pronoun Usage

The influence of systemic racism on pronoun usage is substantial, especially for individuals belonging to marginalized racial groups. Systemic racism encompasses the manner in which societal institutions and structures sustain racial inequality and discrimination. It manifests in various forms, such as discriminatory practices in housing, education, employment, healthcare, and the criminal justice system.

One consequence of systemic racism on pronoun usage is the lack of representation and visibility of individuals from marginalized racial groups in mainstream media and society. This dearth of representation poses challenges for individuals from these groups in finding role models or representation that align with their gender identity. Additionally, it contributes to a limited understanding and acceptance of non-binary and gender non-conforming individuals.

Moreover, systemic racism hinders individuals from marginalized racial groups from accessing resources and information about pronoun usage. This includes obstacles in accessing education, healthcare, and social services, as well as the underrepresentation of these groups in organizations and resources that provide information about pronoun usage.

Furthermore, individuals from marginalized racial groups may encounter discrimination and bias based on both their race/ethnicity and gender identity. This compound effect intensifies the difficulty in expressing their gender identity and being recognized in a manner that aligns with it.

Recognizing the impact of systemic racism on pronoun usage is crucial, and efforts should be made to dismantle the systems that perpetuate it. This involves implementing policies and laws that address racial inequality and discrimination, as well as investing in programs and resources that support individuals from marginalized racial groups.

In conclusion, systemic racism significantly influences pronoun usage, particularly for individuals from marginalized racial groups, through the lack of representation, visibility, access to resources and information, and the compounded effects of discrimination and bias. It is essential to acknowledge this impact and actively work towards dismantling the systems that perpetuate systemic racism, including the implementation of policies and laws that address racial inequality and discrimination, and the allocation of resources to support individuals from marginalized racial groups.

Significance Of Cultural Competency

The concept of cultural competency revolves around an individual's capacity to comprehend, value, and interact effectively with people from diverse cultural backgrounds. Its significance becomes evident when discussing pronoun usage, as various cultures may possess distinct understandings of gender and pronoun norms.

For instance, certain cultures may recognize more than two genders or employ different pronouns than those commonly acknowledged in Western societies. By embodying cultural competency, individuals can enhance their understanding and respect for the diverse ways in which individuals express their gender identity, fostering a more inclusive and equitable environment for everyone involved.

Furthermore, cultural competency plays a vital role in addressing the impact of systemic racism and discrimination on pronoun usage. By acknowledging and respecting the cultural and linguistic diversity of various racial and ethnic groups, individuals can actively contribute to the creation of inclusive and equitable environments for individuals belonging to marginalized racial groups.

Cultural competency also finds relevance in workplace and professional settings. It enables employers to establish inclusive policies and procedures that cater to the needs of a diverse workforce. Additionally, healthcare providers and other professionals can benefit from cultural competency by gaining a better understanding of the diverse ways in which their patients or clients may express their gender identity, ultimately facilitating a more respectful and empathetic approach to care.

In conclusion, cultural competency holds significant importance in pronoun usage as it empowers individuals to comprehend, value, and interact effectively with individuals from diverse cultural backgrounds. By embracing cultural competency, we can cultivate a more inclusive and equitable environment for all, particularly for marginalized racial groups and those whose cultural backgrounds may entail distinct understandings of gender and pronoun usage. Additionally, cultural competency can be applied in professional settings to establish inclusive policies, procedures, and to foster an understanding and respect for the diverse expressions of gender identity among patients and clients.

Conclusion

To conclude, pronoun usage is a multifaceted and intricate subject intimately connected to an individual's gender identity. Understanding the distinct experiences and obstacles encountered by various groups, such as LGBTQ+ individuals, individuals with disabilities, individuals from marginalized racial groups, and individuals from diverse cultural backgrounds, is essential. These groups often confront discrimination, marginalization, and other barriers that can hinder their ability to express their gender identity and receive recognition aligned with their identity.

Recognizing the intersectionality of different identities and experiences and its impact on pronoun usage is crucial. Additionally, acknowledging the influence of systemic discrimination and marginalization, such as systemic racism, on pronoun usage is vital, and it requires proactive efforts to dismantle these systemic structures.

Cultural competency holds significance in pronoun usage as it enables individuals to comprehend, respect, and effectively collaborate with people from diverse cultural backgrounds. It contributes to the creation of a more inclusive and equitable environment for all individuals, particularly those belonging to marginalized racial groups and those whose cultural backgrounds entail distinct understandings of gender and pronoun usage.

To honor and affirm the gender identities of all individuals, it is paramount to employ appropriate pronouns and foster a culture that embraces acceptance and respect for everyone, irrespective of their gender identity.

Summary Of Key Points

The correlation between gender and pronouns is significant, and it is crucial to comprehend the distinct experiences and obstacles faced by various groups, including LGBTQ+ individuals, individuals with disabilities, individuals from marginalized racial groups, and individuals from diverse cultural backgrounds. Understanding the intersectionality of different identities and experiences is essential in relation to pronoun usage.

The impact of systemic discrimination and marginalization, such as systemic racism, can be profound when it comes to pronoun usage. It is imperative to actively strive towards dismantling these systems of oppression. Additionally, cultural competency plays a pivotal role in pronoun usage as it enables individuals to understand, respect, and effectively engage with people from diverse cultural backgrounds.

Sustained education and awareness regarding the intersectionality of gender and pronouns are vital for fostering a more inclusive and equitable environment. This encompasses addressing the consequences of systemic discrimination and marginalization, cultivating an inclusive and accepting culture, promoting effective communication and understanding among individuals with diverse identities and experiences, and mitigating the risk of discrimination, harassment, and other forms of mistreatment against individuals whose gender identity may not align with societal norms. Using appropriate pronouns is paramount in order to demonstrate respect and affirm the gender identities of all individuals.

Intersectionality Of Gender And Pronouns

Sustained education and understanding regarding the intersectionality of gender and pronouns hold great significance for several reasons. Firstly, gaining insight into the experiences and challenges faced by different groups fosters a more inclusive and equitable environment for all individuals. This encompasses understanding the unique experiences of LGBTQ+ individuals, individuals with disabilities, individuals from marginalized racial groups, and individuals from diverse cultural backgrounds.

Furthermore, continuous education and understanding play a crucial role in addressing the impact of systemic discrimination and marginalization on pronoun usage. By comprehending how systemic racism can affect pronoun usage for individuals from marginalized racial groups, it becomes possible to develop more inclusive and equitable policies and practices.

Moreover, ongoing education and understanding contribute to the creation of an inclusive and accepting culture. This involves educating others about the importance of using appropriate pronouns and cultivating a culture that embraces respect and acceptance for all individuals, irrespective of their gender identity.

In addition, continuous education and understanding enhance communication and comprehension between individuals with different identities and experiences. This includes recognizing and respecting the diverse ways in which people express their gender identity, while remaining sensitive to the needs and preferences of individuals with disabilities.

Ultimately, education and understanding help diminish the risk of discrimination, harassment, and other forms of mistreatment against individuals whose gender identity may not conform to societal norms.

In conclusion, continued education and understanding regarding the intersectionality of gender and pronouns are crucial for establishing a more inclusive and equitable environment. This encompasses addressing the impact of systemic discrimination and marginalization, fostering an inclusive and accepting culture, improving communication and understanding among individuals with diverse identities and experiences, and mitigating the risk of discrimination, harassment, and mistreatment against individuals whose gender identity may deviate from societal norms.

Respect And Affirmation Of Gender Identities

In our ongoing pursuit of a more inclusive and just society, it is of utmost importance that we dedicate ourselves to understanding and honoring the unique experiences and identities of individuals, especially in relation to pronoun usage.

Therefore, we urge every individual to actively embrace the use of appropriate pronouns for all, irrespective of their gender identity. This entails educating ourselves about diverse gender identities and pronoun usage, while remaining receptive to the narratives and perspectives of marginalized and underrepresented groups.

Additionally, we implore organizations and institutions to establish policies and practices that foster inclusivity and equity for all individuals, particularly those who encounter discrimination or marginalization based on their gender identity or pronoun usage. This encompasses providing education and training on pronoun usage, as well as cultivating a culture that embraces acceptance and respect for every individual.

Moreover, we call upon individuals and organizations to actively dismantle systemic discrimination and marginalization, such as systemic racism, which can impede pronoun usage for marginalized groups.

In conclusion, by actively striving to use appropriate pronouns and implementing inclusive policies and practices, we can take significant strides towards respecting and affirming the gender identities of all individuals, particularly those whose experiences and identities may have been marginalized or overlooked.

Creating Inclusive Language And Society

Pronouns hold immense significance in fostering an inclusive language and society. By utilizing appropriate pronouns for individuals, we demonstrate our affirmation and respect for their gender identity, cultivating a culture of acceptance and comprehension.

The importance of inclusive language lies in its ability to establish a society where everyone feels acknowledged, valued, and respected. By employing appropriate pronouns, we convey the message that every individual's gender identity is valid and deserving of recognition. This contributes to reducing the risks associated with discrimination, harassment, and other forms of mistreatment faced by those whose gender identity may not conform to societal norms.

Moreover, the use of appropriate pronouns contributes to creating a more inclusive society by challenging and dismantling the societal expectation that one's gender should be immediately discernible or visible. By doing so, we foster a society that embraces and understands the fluidity and intricacy of gender identity.

Inclusive language also fosters an inclusive society by enhancing communication and understanding between individuals from diverse backgrounds and identities. This encompasses recognizing and respecting the various ways in which individuals express their gender identity and exhibiting sensitivity to the needs and preferences of individuals with disabilities.

To conclude, the role of pronouns in cultivating inclusive language and society cannot be overstated. By employing appropriate pronouns, we validate and honor the gender identities of all individuals, while nurturing a culture of acceptance and understanding. Simultaneously, we challenge societal expectations, dismantle systemic discrimination, and enhance communication and comprehension among individuals with distinct identities and experiences. Pronouns are a foundational component of language and communication, playing a pivotal role in shaping our perspectives and interactions regarding gender.

Creating Inclusive Language In Society

The discussion surrounding the role of pronouns in shaping an inclusive language and society centers on the recognition of the significance of employing appropriate pronouns to honor and validate individuals' gender identities. It also encompasses an exploration of how various identities and experiences intersect and influence pronoun usage, emphasizing the crucial role of inclusive language in fostering a fair and inclusive society.

In today's society, this topic holds particular relevance as awareness grows regarding the significance of gender inclusivity and the impact of language on shaping societal norms. The use of appropriate pronouns serves as an act of respect and affirmation for individuals' gender identities, thereby contributing to the reduction of discrimination and marginalization.

Moreover, this topic delves into the examination of how pronoun usage intersects with different identities, such as race, disabilities, and sexual orientation, and how this intersectionality can affect marginalized communities. Understanding the influence of systemic discrimination and marginalization on pronoun usage is essential, as it allows for a critical examination of societal expectations and paves the way for challenging and dismantling these expectations and systemic discrimination through the power of inclusive language.

In conclusion, the topic surrounding the role of pronouns in creating inclusive language and society revolves around recognizing the importance of employing appropriate pronouns. It further encompasses an exploration of how diverse identities and experiences intersect and shape pronoun usage, ultimately highlighting the pivotal role that inclusive language plays in fostering an equitable and inclusive society.

Impact Of Language On Inclusivity And Diversity

The importance of understanding the impact of language on inclusivity and diversity lies in recognizing its influential role in shaping our thoughts and interactions. Language holds tremendous power, and the words we choose and how we use them can significantly affect how individuals and groups are perceived and treated within society.

By employing inclusive language, we contribute to the creation of a more equitable and accepting society. Inclusivity involves acknowledging and valuing the diverse identities and experiences of individuals. This encompasses the use of appropriate pronouns to honor and affirm their gender identities, as well as challenging and dismantling stereotypes and discrimination through mindful language usage when referring to marginalized groups.

Furthermore, comprehending the impact of language on inclusivity and diversity fosters the development of a more inclusive and respectful environment for individuals from diverse backgrounds. This includes an understanding of the different linguistic practices and interpretations among individuals from varied cultures, races, sexual orientations, and abilities. Sensitivity to these differences allows us to cultivate a society that is more inclusive and fair.

Additionally, understanding the impact of language on inclusivity and diversity promotes a society that is well-informed and educated. It raises awareness about how language can perpetuate systemic discrimination and marginalization, while emphasizing the role of inclusive language in dismantling these oppressive systems.

In conclusion, a comprehensive understanding of the impact of language on inclusivity and diversity is vital for establishing a more inclusive, equitable, and respectful society. It necessitates recognizing the power of language in shaping our perceptions and interactions, and being cognizant of how language is used to describe marginalized groups and individuals.

The Power Of Language

The impact of language, specifically regarding gender pronouns, is profound as it molds societal norms and influences our perception of gender. Employing appropriate pronouns to honor and validate individuals' gender identities is pivotal in fostering a more inclusive society. This practice contributes to reducing discrimination and marginalization faced by individuals who do not conform to traditional binary gender norms.

By referring to individuals with pronouns that align with their gender identity, we affirm their sense of self and foster a sense of belonging and validation within society. Conversely, misusing pronouns that do not align with an individual's gender identity can lead to feelings of alienation and invalidation. Such experiences can have adverse effects on an individual's mental and emotional well-being, perpetuating a culture of discrimination and marginalization.

Furthermore, language holds significant influence in shaping societal norms and perceptions of gender. The use of inclusive language and non-binary pronouns serves to challenge and dismantle societal expectations and stereotypes surrounding gender. This active effort helps in creating a more inclusive and equitable society that respects and recognizes individuals of all gender identities.

In conclusion, the power of language concerning gender pronouns is substantial as it molds societal norms, shapes perceptions, and impacts how individuals are treated within society. By utilizing appropriate pronouns, we contribute to the establishment of a more inclusive society, diminishing discrimination and marginalization faced by individuals who do not conform to traditional binary gender norms. Embracing inclusive language and non-binary pronouns further aids in challenging and dismantling societal expectations and stereotypes surrounding gender.

Language And Societal Perception Connection

Language serves as a vital link to societal perceptions as it forms the primary medium through which we communicate and comprehend our own experiences and those of others. The choice of words, phrases, and grammar in our language significantly influences our understanding of the world and its inhabitants.

For instance, language can perpetuate societal stereotypes when certain groups, like women, are consistently portrayed as emotional or weak, while men are depicted as strong and unemotional. This reinforcement of harmful stereotypes within society can contribute to discrimination and marginalization.

Furthermore, language can establish and reinforce power dynamics and systems of oppression. When language is used to dehumanize or belittle specific groups, such as through racial slurs, it perpetuates racism and discrimination. Similarly, language that reinforces gender stereotypes can perpetuate sexism and discrimination against individuals with non-binary gender identities.

Conversely, inclusive language and the use of non-binary pronouns play a vital role in challenging and dismantling societal stereotypes and oppressive systems. In employing inclusive language, we acknowledge and appreciate the diverse identities and experiences of individuals. By using non-binary pronouns, we confront societal expectations that demand immediate legibility or visibility of one's gender.

In conclusion, language intricately connects to societal perceptions, and the words we choose hold tremendous power in shaping our understanding and interactions with the world. While language can reinforce damaging stereotypes and oppressive systems, it can also be harnessed to challenge and dismantle these very structures. By embracing inclusive language, we contribute to the creation of a more just and accepting society.

Impact On Shaping Attitudes And Beliefs

Language holds immense power in shaping our attitudes and beliefs, influencing our understanding and interactions with the world and others. It also plays a pivotal role in shaping our perceptions and beliefs about ourselves and our identities.

For instance, language can contribute to discrimination and marginalization when it reinforces harmful stereotypes. When language is used to belittle or dehumanize certain groups, such as through racial slurs, it perpetuates racist attitudes and beliefs. Likewise, the use of language that reinforces gender stereotypes perpetuates sexism and discrimination against individuals with non-binary gender identities.

Conversely, the use of inclusive language fosters more positive attitudes and beliefs. By employing language that acknowledges and values diversity, we can engage with people from different backgrounds and experiences in a respectful and equitable manner. Additionally, using non-binary pronouns challenges societal expectations that demand immediate categorization of gender, leading to more accepting attitudes towards individuals with non-binary gender identities.

Furthermore, language also shapes our self-perception and beliefs about ourselves. When our gender identity is affirmed through the use of appropriate pronouns, it fosters a sense of belonging and validation within society. Conversely, misalignment between our gender identity and the pronouns used can generate feelings of alienation and invalidation, negatively impacting our mental and emotional well-being.

In conclusion, language significantly influences our attitudes and beliefs, impacting our understanding of the world, our interactions with others, and our own self-perception. Employing inclusive language and embracing non-binary pronouns promotes positive attitudes and beliefs about diversity, equity, and acceptance.

Role Of Language In Creating Discrimination

Language wields substantial influence in the creation and perpetuation of discrimination. The manner in which we utilize language shapes our comprehension of the world and its inhabitants, while also establishing and reinforcing systems of power and oppression.

For instance, the use of language that belittles or dehumanizes certain groups, such as racial slurs, serves to sustain racism and discrimination. Similarly, language that reinforces gender stereotypes contributes to sexism and discrimination against individuals with non-binary gender identities.

Moreover, discriminatory language erects barriers for marginalized communities. When individuals with disabilities are deprived of accessible language options, their full participation in society is hindered. Likewise, when non-English speakers lack access to translation services, they may be denied critical information and resources.

Furthermore, discriminatory language molds societal norms and fosters expectations that perpetuate marginalization and discrimination. By perpetuating harmful stereotypes, language shapes societal expectations that can lead to discrimination and marginalization of those who deviate from these stereotypes.

Conversely, inclusive language assumes a vital role in dismantling discrimination and forging a more equitable society. Through its implementation, individuals can recognize and value the diverse identities and experiences of others. Likewise, the use of non-binary pronouns challenges societal expectations that demand immediate categorization of gender, thus fostering a more inclusive society.

In conclusion, language occupies a significant role in the creation and perpetuation of discrimination. The manner in which we employ language can establish and reinforce systems of power and oppression, perpetuate detrimental stereotypes and societal norms, as well as construct barriers for marginalized communities. Nevertheless, the adoption of inclusive language and non-binary pronouns plays a crucial role in dismantling discrimination and cultivating a more equitable society.

The Role Of Pronouns In Inclusive Language

The role of pronouns in fostering inclusive language is of utmost importance. Pronouns, as a fundamental component of our language, serve the purpose of referring to and identifying individuals. However, their usage also influences our understanding of gender identities and expressions, ultimately shaping whether our language is inclusive or exclusive.

When individuals are addressed with pronouns that align with their gender identity, it affirms their sense of self, fostering a feeling of belonging and validation within society. Conversely, when individuals are referred to using pronouns that do not align with their gender identity, it can lead to feelings of alienation and invalidation. This can significantly impact their mental and emotional well-being, as well as their overall sense of identity.

In addition, the utilization of non-binary pronouns contributes to the creation of inclusive language. Non-binary pronouns are employed by individuals who identify as non-binary, meaning they do not exclusively identify as male or female. Incorporating non-binary pronouns helps in acknowledging and affirming non-binary identities while challenging societal expectations that insist on gender being immediately apparent or visible.

Furthermore, inclusive language plays a pivotal role in establishing a more equitable society. By employing language that recognizes and values the diverse identities and experiences of individuals, we foster an environment of respect and fairness for everyone.

In conclusion, the significance of pronouns in shaping inclusive language cannot be overstated. By utilizing pronouns that align with individuals' gender identities and incorporating non-binary pronouns, we validate and affirm their identities. Simultaneously, by embracing inclusive language, we cultivate an environment characterized by respect and equity for all individuals.

Pronouns In Language And Communication

Pronouns hold a significant place in language and communication as they serve to identify and refer to individuals. They are an essential component of our daily linguistic interactions, playing a pivotal role in how we perceive and engage with one another.

One of the primary reasons why pronouns are important lies in their ability to establish and nurture social connections. When we utilize the appropriate pronouns to address someone, we convey respect and acknowledgment of their identity, both to them and those around us. This contributes to building trust, fostering understanding, and promoting positive interactions. Conversely, using incorrect pronouns can result in feelings of exclusion, disrespect, and strain on relationships.

Moreover, pronouns play a crucial role in shaping our comprehension of gender identities and expressions. The manner in which we employ pronouns can either reinforce or challenge societal expectations and norms regarding gender, thereby influencing the inclusivity or exclusivity of our society.

Furthermore, pronouns also exert an impact on individuals' mental and emotional well-being. When individuals are referred to using pronouns that align with their gender identity, it affirms their sense of self, cultivating a sense of belonging and validation within society. Conversely, being addressed with pronouns that do not align with their gender identity can generate feelings of alienation and invalidation.

Additionally, in the realm of communication, pronouns contribute to efficiency and accuracy. They enable us to reference previously mentioned nouns or individuals without the need for repetitive naming.

In conclusion, pronouns hold immense significance in language and communication. They aid in the identification and reference of individuals, foster social relationships, shape our understanding of gender identities and expressions, impact mental and emotional well-being, and enhance communication efficiency and accuracy.

Impact Of Inclusive Pronoun Usage

The utilization of inclusive pronouns, including non-binary pronouns, holds immense potential for fostering a more equitable society. When language is employed to acknowledge and appreciate the multitude of identities and expressions individuals possess, it cultivates an environment that is both respectful and inclusive, benefiting all members of society.

One of the primary ways in which inclusive pronoun usage contributes to a more equitable society is by challenging and dismantling societal norms and expectations surrounding gender. The use of non-binary pronouns serves to recognize and validate non-binary identities, effectively challenging the assumption that gender should be immediately discernible or confined to traditional categories. This fosters a more inclusive and equitable society that embraces the diversity of all genders.

Moreover, inclusive pronoun usage plays a pivotal role in establishing an inclusive and accepting society for transgender and gender non-conforming individuals. When individuals are addressed using pronouns that align with their gender identity, it affirms their sense of self and fosters a deep sense of belonging and validation within society. By doing so, it helps to combat discrimination, marginalization, and violence that disproportionately affect transgender and gender non-conforming individuals.

Furthermore, inclusive pronoun usage extends its impact to the realm of work and education, cultivating an inclusive and respectful environment. Employing correct pronouns demonstrates a commitment to respect and inclusivity, thereby fostering a more productive and harmonious work atmosphere for all. This, in turn, contributes to enhanced employee satisfaction, increased productivity, and improved retention rates.

In conclusion, the use of inclusive pronouns, such as non-binary pronouns, holds significant potential in cultivating a more equitable society. By recognizing and affirming the diverse identities and expressions of individuals, it fosters an inclusive, respectful, and equitable environment. This serves to challenge societal norms, diminish discrimination and marginalization, and establish a more inclusive and respectful work and educational landscape.

Role Of Pronouns For All Gender Identities

The utilization of inclusive pronouns, including non-binary pronouns, plays a vital role in fostering respect and affirmation for all gender identities. When language is employed to acknowledge and value the diverse range of identities and expressions individuals possess, it cultivates an environment that is more respectful and inclusive for everyone.

One of the primary ways in which inclusive pronoun usage promotes respect and affirmation for all gender identities is by challenging and dismantling societal norms and expectations surrounding gender. By incorporating non-binary pronouns, it recognizes and validates non-binary identities, effectively challenging the societal expectation that gender should be immediately discernible or confined within traditional categories. This helps to create a more inclusive and equitable society that embraces and respects all genders.

Moreover, inclusive pronoun usage contributes to creating a more inclusive and accepting society for transgender and gender non-conforming individuals. When individuals are addressed using pronouns that align with their gender identity, it affirms their identity and fosters a sense of belonging and validation within society. This, in turn, helps to reduce discrimination, marginalization, and violence that disproportionately affect transgender and gender non-conforming individuals.

Furthermore, inclusive pronoun usage promotes respect and affirmation for all gender identities by facilitating education and raising awareness about the importance of pronoun usage. Through education and awareness efforts, individuals can learn to be more mindful and respectful of the pronouns used by others, as well as develop an understanding of the significance of inclusive pronoun usage. This, in turn, contributes to the creation of a more respectful and accepting society for all.

In conclusion, using inclusive pronouns plays a critical role in promoting respect and affirmation for all gender identities. By recognizing and affirming the diverse range of individuals' identities and expressions, it creates a more inclusive, respectful, and equitable environment for everyone. This helps to challenge societal norms, reduce discrimination and marginalization, and foster a society that is more inclusive and respectful of all gender identities.

Building Inclusive Communities

The process of building inclusive communities involves creating a safe and welcoming environment that embraces individuals from all backgrounds and identities. This entails actively confronting and challenging systems of oppression and discrimination, while providing space for underrepresented and marginalized groups to express themselves and have their needs recognized.

Addressing and challenging systems of oppression, such as racism, sexism, ableism, and homophobia, is a crucial component of building inclusive communities. This involves educating oneself and others about these issues and taking proactive steps to combat them in personal and professional spheres.

Creating opportunities for underrepresented and marginalized groups to have their voices heard and their needs addressed is another important aspect of building inclusive communities. This entails actively seeking out and amplifying the perspectives and experiences of marginalized groups, as well as establishing safe spaces where individuals can openly share their viewpoints.

Language and communication play a significant role in fostering inclusive communities. This encompasses using inclusive language, including non-binary pronouns, and being mindful of how language shapes attitudes and beliefs about marginalized groups.

Inclusive communities also involve implementing policies and practices that support diversity, equity, and inclusion. This includes promoting equal opportunities through policy frameworks, ensuring accessibility for individuals with disabilities in workplaces or organizations, and providing comprehensive training on unconscious bias to all community members.

In conclusion, building inclusive communities requires proactive efforts to address and challenge systems of oppression, provide platforms for underrepresented groups to be heard, and establish policies and practices that uphold diversity, equity, and inclusion. It necessitates continuous education, self-reflection, and a steadfast commitment to fostering a safe and welcoming environment for all individuals.

Inclusive Language On Creating Communities

Inclusive language serves as a critical tool in establishing inclusive communities, as it cultivates respect and affirmation for individuals irrespective of their backgrounds or identities. By employing inclusive language, including the use of non-binary pronouns, communities can acknowledge and validate the diverse identities and experiences of their members.

The use of inclusive language sends a powerful message to marginalized and underrepresented groups, assuring them that their presence is acknowledged, their voices are heard, and their worth is recognized within the community. This fosters a sense of belonging, acceptance, and safety, enabling individuals to feel more at ease in sharing their unique perspectives and experiences.

Conversely, the use of language that perpetuates systems of oppression, such as discriminatory or derogatory language, contributes to an environment that is hostile and unwelcoming for marginalized groups. This further marginalizes and isolates individuals, hindering their full participation and benefit from the community.

Inclusive language also plays a pivotal role in shaping societal perceptions and attitudes towards marginalized groups. By employing language that acknowledges and validates diverse identities and experiences, communities can challenge and transform societal norms and stereotypes.

To establish truly inclusive communities, it is essential to recognize the power of language and proactively incorporate inclusive language in all forms of communication. This entails being mindful of language choices in conversations, written materials, and policies, and actively striving to challenge and alter language that perpetuates systems of oppression.

In conclusion, inclusive language holds a critical role in creating inclusive communities by fostering respect and affirmation for all individuals, cultivating a sense of belonging and acceptance, and influencing societal perceptions and attitudes towards marginalized groups. Achieving this necessitates continuous education and a steadfast commitment to employing language that acknowledges and validates the diverse identities and experiences of every individual.

Tips For Promoting Inclusivity In Language Usage

Promoting inclusivity in language usage involves several valuable tips:

To begin, using gender-neutral or non-binary pronouns, like they/them/theirs, can foster inclusivity. This approach recognizes and affirms the diverse identities and experiences of individuals whose pronouns are unknown or who identify as non-binary.

In conversations, it is essential to be mindful of the language employed, particularly when discussing marginalized or underrepresented groups. Avoiding language that perpetuates systems of oppession, such as discriminatory or derogatory terms, contributes to a more inclusive environment.

Continuously educating yourself and others about the impact of language on inclusivity and diversity is crucial. This involves understanding different identities and experiences, as well as delving into the historical context and meaning behind certain words and phrases.

Remaining open to feedback and being willing to adjust your language usage is key. If someone informs you that something you said or wrote was hurtful or offensive, it is important to listen and make necessary changes.

Encouraging others to use inclusive language and actively recognizing and validating diverse identities and experiences is a powerful way to promote inclusivity.

When using language, being sensitive to the context, culture, and surrounding environment is paramount. This entails understanding the impact of words, idioms, and phrases across different cultures and situations.

In written materials and policies, employing inclusive language by avoiding gendered terms and embracing gender-neutral alternatives ensures that all individuals feel included and respected in all forms of communication.

Lastly, practicing active listening involves attentively and empathetically engaging with others' expressions, being open to learning from their perspectives and experiences.

Remember, inclusive language usage is an ongoing commitment. It requires continuous education, unwavering dedication, and a willingness to challenge and transform language that perpetuates oppressive systems.

Appropriate Pronouns Socially And Professionally

Promoting the use of appropriate pronouns in social and professional settings can be achieved through the following tips:

Lead by example by sharing your own pronouns and consistently using the correct pronouns when referring to others. This sets a positive example and encourages others to follow suit.

Provide opportunities for individuals to share their pronouns in various settings, such as introductions, email signatures, or name tags. This fosters a culture of respect and affirmation for all gender identities.

Educate others about the significance of using appropriate pronouns and the impact of misgendering on individuals. This can be accomplished through workshops, training sessions, or informational materials.

Use inclusive language in all forms of communication. This involves avoiding gendered language and opting for gender-neutral terms, contributing to a more inclusive environment for everyone.

Create a safe and inclusive space where individuals can freely express their gender identity and pronouns. Implement policies, procedures, and practices that promote inclusivity and respect for all individuals.

Encourage the utilization of gender-neutral bathrooms and changing rooms, which helps establish an inclusive environment regardless of one's gender identity.

Be receptive to feedback and willing to make adjustments in your language usage. If someone informs you that something you said or wrote was hurtful or offensive, apologize, correct yourself, and commit to using the correct pronouns moving forward.

Promote the inclusion of pronouns in email signatures, name tags, and other forms of identification. This helps cultivate a culture that respects and affirms all gender identities.

Even if you make a mistake, use the correct pronouns and apologize if necessary. Acknowledge the error, correct yourself, and make a conscious effort to use the appropriate pronouns thereafter.

Encourage the use of appropriate pronouns in job interviews and work evaluations to foster a workplace culture that respects and affirms all gender identities.

By implementing these tips, individuals can contribute to a more inclusive environment by promoting the use of appropriate pronouns in various social and professional contexts.

Conclusion

In conclusion, recognizing and using appropriate pronouns is a fundamental aspect of fostering inclusivity in both language and society. By understanding the complex interplay between gender and pronouns and acknowledging the diverse experiences and identities of individuals, we can cultivate an environment that promotes respect and validation for all gender identities. The significant role of pronouns in shaping societal perceptions, attitudes, and beliefs, as well as their potential to perpetuate discrimination, underscores the criticality of embracing inclusive pronoun usage.

To build inclusive communities, it is imperative to prioritize inclusive language usage, provide education and training on pronoun awareness, and establish safe spaces where individuals feel comfortable expressing their identities. These strategies serve as crucial foundations for encouraging the adoption of appropriate pronouns in social and professional settings. Additionally, it is vital for us to remain committed to continuous education and actively work towards creating a more equitable society that embraces and affirms all individuals.

By embracing appropriate pronoun usage, we contribute to the creation of an inclusive language and society that recognizes and respects the diversity of gender identities. It is through our collective efforts that we can foster a sense of belonging and empower individuals to express their authentic selves. Let us strive to create an environment where everyone is seen, heard, and valued.

Summary Of Key Points

In summary, recognizing and using appropriate pronouns is vital for fostering inclusive language and society. Pronouns hold significant influence in shaping societal perceptions of gender identity and expression. Understanding the intersectionality of gender and pronouns is crucial to promote respect and validation for all gender identities. Moreover, we must acknowledge the profound impact language has on attitudes, beliefs, and the perpetuation of discrimination. By advocating for inclusive language and pronoun usage, we can actively contribute to the construction of inclusive communities where everyone feels valued and respected. However, it is crucial to embrace a continuous journey of education and be open to learning and adapting. It is our collective responsibility to take tangible steps in all spheres of society to promote inclusivity through appropriate pronoun usage.

Here are the key takeaways for fostering inclusive communities through language:

Pronouns hold significant influence in shaping societal perceptions of gender identity and expression.

Recognizing and using appropriate pronouns is vital for creating inclusive language and society.

Understanding the intersectionality of gender and pronouns, including the experiences of marginalized communities, is crucial for fostering respect and validation for all gender identities.

Acknowledging the impact of language on attitudes, beliefs, and the perpetuation of discrimination is essential.

Embracing inclusive language and pronoun usage contributes to the formation of inclusive communities.

Continuous education and a willingness to learn and adapt are integral to promoting inclusivity through pronoun usage.

Taking action to promote inclusivity through the use of appropriate pronouns in workplaces, schools, and community spaces is paramount.

Importance Of Continued Education

The significance of ongoing education and comprehending the role of pronouns in establishing inclusive language and society cannot be emphasized enough. As societal norms and understanding evolve, it becomes crucial to stay updated on current best practices and language usage. Moreover, as individuals, we need to be receptive to learning and expanding our understanding of others' experiences and identities. Only by continuously educating ourselves and fostering understanding can we actively contribute to the creation of a more inclusive language and society. This entails being open to feedback and being willing to modify our own pronoun usage to cultivate a more inclusive environment for those around us. It is an ongoing endeavor that demands commitment and dedication to building a fair and equitable society for everyone.

Promotion Of Inclusivity

In society, it is imperative that we take decisive steps to promote inclusivity by utilizing appropriate pronouns in all domains. This encompasses various actions, including but not limited to:

Encouraging the use of preferred pronouns in both professional and social settings, such as introductions, email signatures, and name tags.

Fostering a culture that values and asks for individuals' preferred pronouns in all settings, including workplaces, schools, and community spaces.

Providing comprehensive training and education on pronoun usage and inclusivity for employees, students, and community members.

Incorporating inclusive language and pronoun options in forms, documents, and official communications.

Taking a stand against discrimination and marginalization based on pronoun usage and gender identity.

Amplifying the voices and experiences of marginalized communities and offering support.

It is crucial to remain open to feedback and be willing to adjust our own pronoun usage in order to create an environment that fosters inclusivity for those around us.

Together, we can strive towards establishing a society that respects and affirms all gender identities through the appropriate use of pronouns. It is our collective responsibility to take action and commit ourselves to building a more inclusive and equitable society for everyone.

In conclusion, this book has explored the significance of using gender pronouns correctly as a means of demonstrating respect and affirming individual identities. We have delved into the importance of comprehending the intersectionality of gender and pronouns, including the distinct experiences of marginalized communities. Moreover, we have examined the impact of language in shaping attitudes, beliefs, and the creation of discrimination. By promoting inclusive language and employing appropriate pronouns, we can work towards the creation of inclusive communities where everyone feels acknowledged and validated. We hope that this book has enhanced the understanding of the importance of utilizing appropriate pronouns and its role in fostering inclusivity and respect for all individuals. It is our responsibility to take action by using appropriate pronouns in every facet of society. Let us all strive to employ gender pronouns correctly and contribute to building a more inclusive world for everyone.